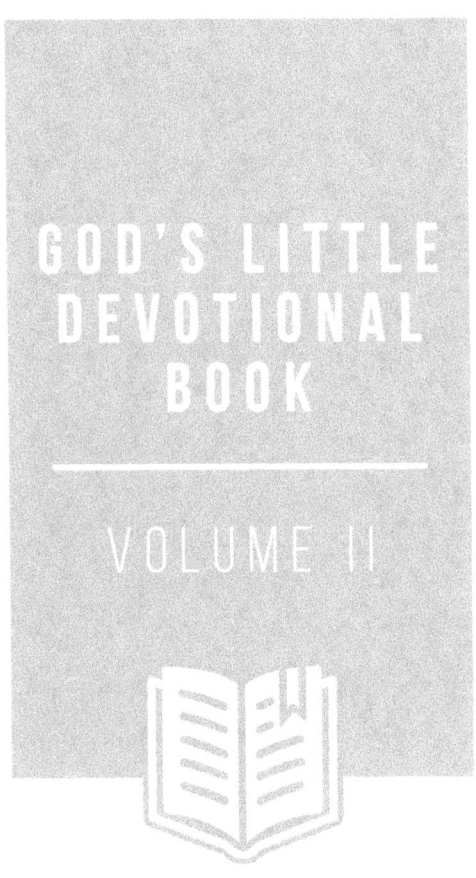

GOD'S LITTLE DEVOTIONAL BOOK

VOLUME II

RACINE, WI

God's Little Devotional Book - Volume 2
ISBN: 979-8-88898-159-7 - *Paperback*
ISBN: 979-8-88898-160-3 - *Hardcover*
ISBN: 979-8-88898-161-0 - *Ebook*
Copyright © 2024 by Honor Books, Racine, WI

INTRODUCTION

A Daily Blessing...

   We take our daily vitamins.

We read, watch, or listen to the news every day.

We try to exercise daily.

We bathe or shower daily.

And, we know the value of reading the Word of God daily.

Most of us have some kind of daily routine. Indeed, the Word of God admonishes us to live our lives "one day at a time"—sufficient unto each day are that day's problems, and adequate for each day is the "daily bread" which God supplies. When we master our daily disciplines, we gain mastery over our lives.

One of the best habits you can build into your daily routine is reading something designed to motivate you to live out a life of high moral character and demonstrative faith.

This book is just that—a tool for daily self-motivation, a means of reminding yourself of the values, attitudes, beliefs, and behaviors that you not only know to be good, but which you desire to manifest in your life. Make *God's Little Devotional Book Volume II* your key to a daily blessing!

CHOICE, NOT CHANCE, DETERMINES HUMAN DESTINY.

Victor Frankl was a psychiatrist and a Jew. While imprisoned in the death camps of Nazi Germany, he suffered unthinkable torture and innumerable indignities. His parents, brother, and wife all died in the camp or were sent to the gas chamber. Frankl never knew from one moment to the next if his path would lead to the ovens, or if he would be among the "saved" who were forced to shovel the ashes of the ill-fated.

One day, alone and naked in a small room, Frankl became aware of what he later called "the last of the human freedoms"—the control over his inner environment and his basic identity. *He could decide within himself how all of this was going to affect him.* Through a series of mental, emotional, and moral disciplines—largely using memory and imagination—he exercised this freedom, and it grew.

Eventually, he felt he had more freedom than his captors. They might have had the liberty to make choices in their external environment, but he had more freedom, more internal power. He became an inspiration to the prisoners around him, and even to some of his guards. He helped others find meaning in their suffering and dignity in their prison existence.[1]

Others may determine what happens to you on the outside, but only you and God determine your inside fate.

"I have set before you life and death, blessing and cursing: therefore choose life, that both thou and thy seed may live."

DEUTERONOMY 30:19

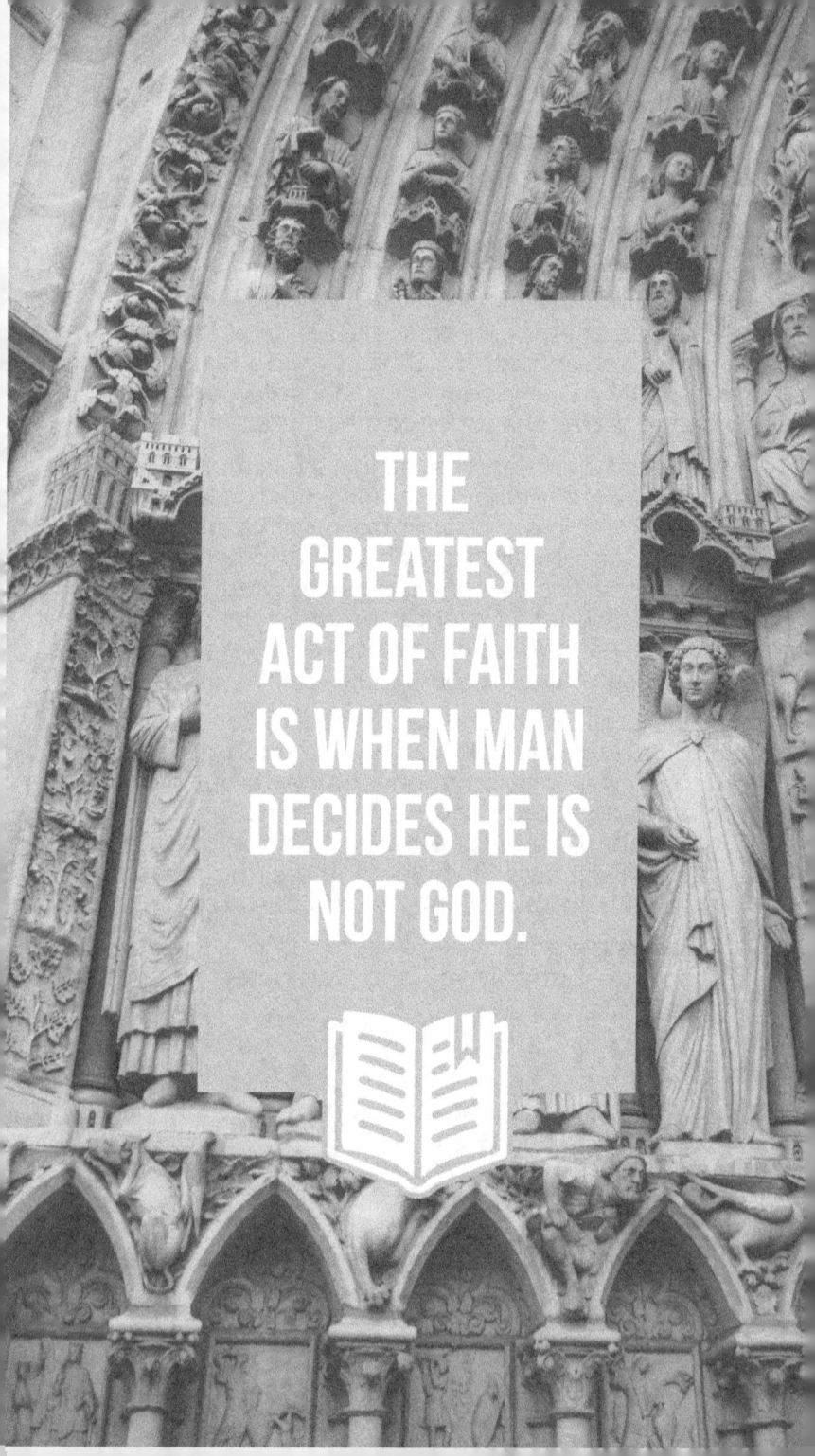

THE GREATEST ACT OF FAITH IS WHEN MAN DECIDES HE IS NOT GOD.

James Hewett has written, "When I recognized this Higher Power, it seemed as though life was rather like a bike ride, but it was a tandem bike . . . God was in the back helping me pedal. I don't know just when it was that He suggested we change places, but life has not been the same since . . . When He took the lead, it was all I could do to hang on! He knew delightful paths, up mountains and through rocky places—and at breakneck speeds.

"I worried and was anxious and asked, 'Where are you taking me?' He laughed and didn't answer, and I started to learn trust. I forgot my boring life and entered into adventure. When I'd say, 'I'm scared,' He'd lean back and touch my hand. He took me to people with gifts . . . of healing, acceptance, and joy. They gave me their gifts to take on my journey, our journey, God's and mine. And we were off again. He said, 'Give the gifts away; they're extra baggage, too much weight.' So I did, to the people we met, and I found that in giving I received . . .

"At first I did not trust Him in control of my life. I thought He'd wreck it, but He knows bike secrets— knows how to make it lean to take sharp corners, dodge large rocks, and speed through scary passages . . . I'm beginning to enjoy the view and the cool breeze on my face with my delightful, constant Companion."[2]

Today, let God take the front seat. Enjoy the ride!

Know ye that the Lord he is God: it is he that hath made us, and not we ourselves; we are his people, and the sheep of his pasture.

PSALM 100:3

SUCCESS IS TO BE
MEASURED NOT SO
MUCH BY THE
POSITION THAT ONE
HAS REACHED IN
LIFE AS BY THE
OBSTACLES WHICH
HE HAS OVERCOME
WHILE TRYING TO
SUCCEED.

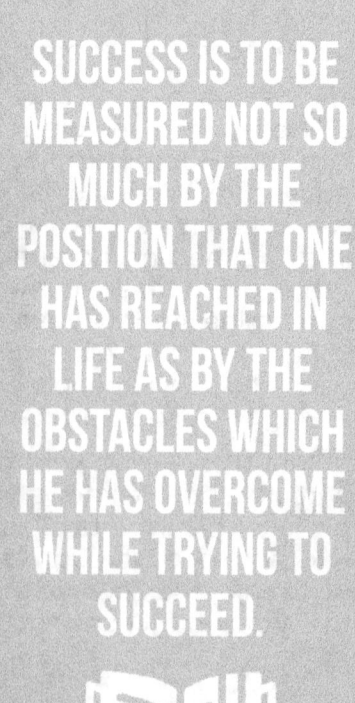

On a trip to Israel, a tourist was amazed to hear a young Jewish man recite his family lineage back fourteen generations. She reflected upon her own family tree, and realized that she could only trace her own lineage back five generations. She concluded, "God is the only one who knows *my* beginning from my ending."

Ultimately, that is true for each person. No one fully knows what another has experienced early in life, or what genetic influences may be brought to bear in a person's life because of the behavior of his or her parents and other ancestors. A part of each person will always remain a mystery, known to God alone.

Don't find fault with the man who limps
Or stumbles along life's road,
Unless you have worn the shoes he wears,
Or struggled beneath his load.

There may be tacks in his shoes that hurt,
Though hidden away from your view,
The burdens he bears, if placed on your back
Might cause you to stumble, too.

Don't be too hard on the man who errs,
Or pelt him with wood or stone,
Unless you are sure—yea, double sure,
That you have no fault of your own.[3]

Blessed is the man who perseveres under trial, because when he has stood the test, he will receive the crown of life that God has promised to those who love him.

JAMES 1:12 NIV

TO BE UPSET
OVER WHAT
YOU DON'T
HAVE IS TO
WASTE WHAT
YOU DO HAVE.

I n *The Fisherman and His Wife*, Lucy Crane tells the story of a fisherman who catches a large fish who is really an enchanted prince. The fisherman lets the prince go free and returns home empty-handed. His wife persuades him to return to the sea and ask the enchanted prince to grant him a wish in return for sparing his life.

He does so, asking (at his wife's request) that their small hut be turned into a cottage. By the time he returns home her wish has been granted. His wife soon tires of the cottage, however, and sends her husband back to ask the fish for a large stone castle. Again, her wish is granted.

After the wife has tired of her castle, she asks to become queen, then to have a palace, to be made an empress, and finally to be made ruler over the sun and moon. At this, the enchanted prince tells the fisherman to return home where he will find his wife back in their old hut.[4]

We can waste an amazing amount of time, energy, and resources wishing for possessions, relationships, and achievements. When we do this, we fail to enjoy God's immediate gifts. God desires that we savor each moment of every day. It is only when we see God in the *now* moments of our lives that we can truly recognize His work in our future.

Because the Lord is my Shepherd,
I have everything I need!

PSALM 23:1 TLB

A TRUE FRIEND
NEVER GETS IN
YOUR WAY
UNLESS YOU
HAPPEN TO BE
GOING DOWN.

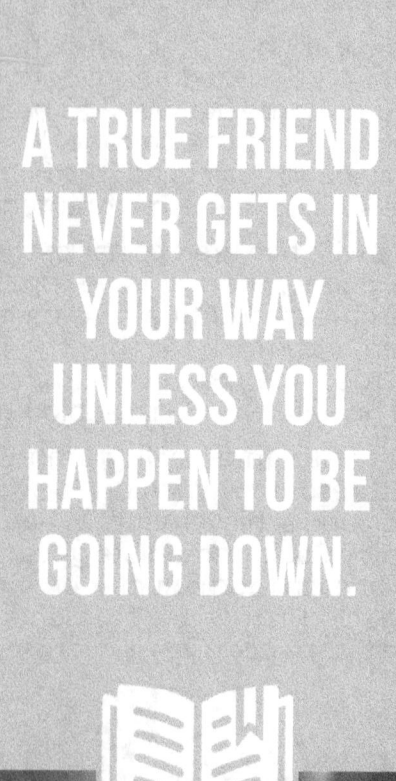

Richard Exley, in *Life's Bottom Line*, writes, "Several weeks ago I was agonizing over a situation in which I had to discipline a man. Though I felt I had done the right thing, and in the right way, I still grieved for him. As I was wrestling with my feelings in prayer, I sensed the Lord speaking to me and I wrote:

"*My son, power is a dangerous thing, and it must always be mitigated with My eternal love. I will cause you to feel the pain of My discipline even when it is toward another. You will feel every sting of the lash in your own flesh. You must, or in your zealousness you would go too far. You will grieve, even as Samuel grieved for Saul. Yet I will also make you feel the awful pain of their sin, for if you do not feel that terrible pain, you will draw back from administering the discipline of the Lord.*'"

Exley concludes, "Confrontation is invariably necessary. A relationship seldom achieves its full potential without it; but it is almost always doomed to failure unless it grows out of a deep trust built on honest communication … It is extremely important to take great care to create a safe place of affirmation and acceptance, where a person can be assured, again and again, of our love. Even then, confrontation will be risky and should be undertaken only after we have carefully prepared our hearts before the Lord."[5]

A friend loves at all times, and a brother is born for adversity.

PROVERBS 17:17 NASB

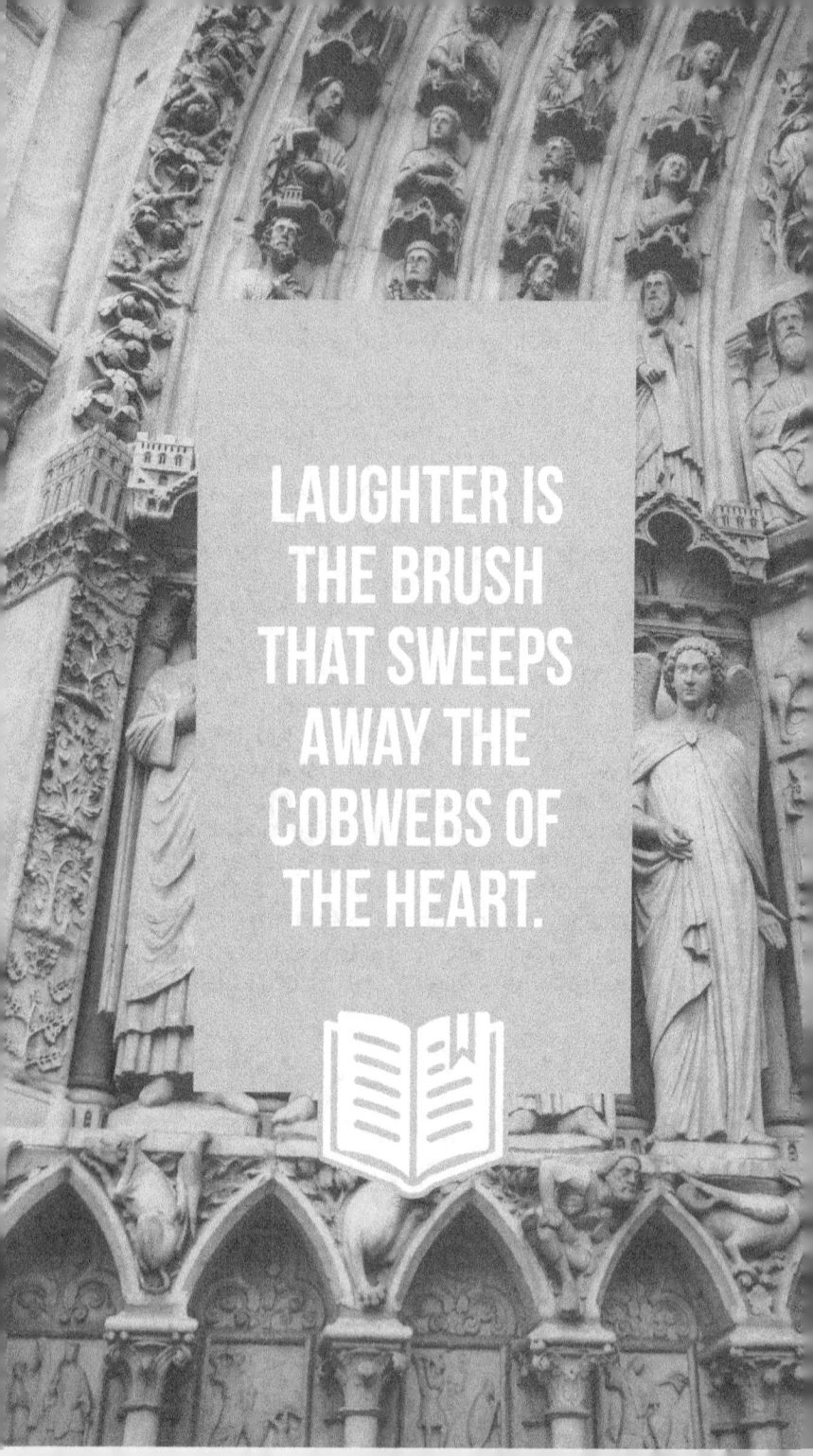

Scientists have studied the effect laughter has on human beings and have found, among other things, that laughter has a profound, instantaneous effect on virtually every important organ in the human body.

Laughter reduces health-sapping tension. It simultaneously relaxes the tissues and exercises the organs. It causes the release of both dopamine and serotonin in the brain, natural substances that contribute to a general feeling of well-being.

Similarly, the great preacher Charles H. Spurgeon once emphasized to a preaching class the importance of making facial expressions that harmonized with one's sermon.

"When you speak of Heaven," he said, "let your face light up, let it be irradiated with a heavenly gleam, let your eyes shine with reflected glory. But when you speak of Hell—well, then your ordinary face will do."[6]

While we may think it contrived to "force" a facial expression, such as a smile, or to force a laugh, scientists have found that even *forced* laughter has a beneficial effect, both mentally and physically.

Next time you feel nervous, tired, or stressed, indulge in a good laugh!

A happy heart is good medicine and a cheerful mind works healing, but a broken spirit dries the bones.

PROVERBS 17:22 AMP

MANY A MAN
THINKS HE HAS
AN OPEN MIND,
WHEN IT'S
MERELY
VACANT.

For more than one hundred years, the Swiss set the standard for excellence in watch-making. In 1968, they held 65 percent of the world market and an estimated 80 percent of the profits. Ten years later, their market share was less than 10 percent. Over the next three years, more than half of the sixty-five thousand watch-makers in Switzerland became unemployed.

Today, the world leader in watchmaking is Japan. In 1968, the Japanese had virtually no share of the watch market. Then, they began to manufacture totally electronic, quartz-movement watches. Far more accurate than mechanical watches, they could run for years on one small battery.

Who invented the quartz-movement watch? The Swiss! Swiss researchers presented the quartz watch to Swiss watchmakers in 1967, but they rejected it, saying it would never work. The watch-makers rejected the idea so soundly that the researchers didn't even protect their idea with a patent. When they later presented their invention at an international watch convention, representatives from Seiko and Texas Instruments jumped on it immediately.[7]

Every invention can be improved upon. Creative ideas, or witty inventions, come from God, and His creativity is infinite!

I warn everyone among you not to estimate and think of himself more highly than he ought [not to have an exaggerated opinion of his own importance].

ROMANS 12:3 AMP

CHARACTER IS NOT MADE IN CRISIS, IT IS ONLY EXHIBITED.

Several years ago on a flight out of Orlando, the pilot recognized that something was amiss the minute the plane took off. He quickly turned back to the Orlando airport and warned the passengers to prepare for a crash landing; the hydraulic system had failed.

The passengers were stunned and visibly frightened. Many began to cry, and some even wailed or screamed. Almost everyone lost their composure in one way or another, but one woman continued to talk in a calm, normal voice. She stared into the face of her four-year-old daughter, who was listening to her intently.

She said, "I love you so much. Do you know I love you more than anything?"

"Yes, Mommy."

The mother continued, "And remember, no matter what happens, that I love you always. And that you are a good girl. Sometimes things happen that are not your fault. You are still a good girl and my love will always be with you."

Then the mother laid over her daughter, strapped the seat belt over both of them, and prepared to crash. The mother's love and character had given her courage. Miraculously, the landing gear held. The plane landed safely.[8]

Character is built layer upon layer, not in one big act. "Having what it takes" for tomorrow will be a direct result of "doing what is right" today.

I have set the Lord always before me: because he is at my right hand, I shall not be moved.

PSALM 16:8

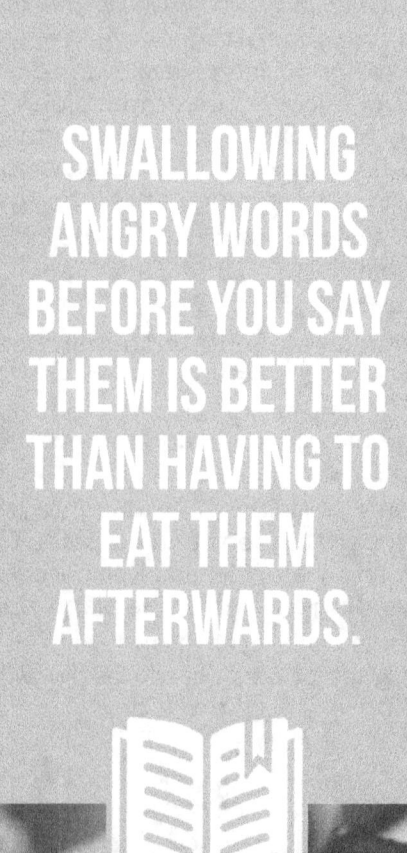

SWALLOWING ANGRY WORDS BEFORE YOU SAY THEM IS BETTER THAN HAVING TO EAT THEM AFTERWARDS.

In the early 1950s, President Truman appointed Newbold Morris to investigate allegations of crime and mismanagement in high levels of government. Just a few months later, Morris was himself in the witness chair in the Senate hearing room answering a barrage of questions from a Senate subcommittee about the sale of some ships by his own New York company.

The investigation was intense and the subcommittee's questions were becoming increasingly accusatory and fierce. Morris' face first recorded pain, then surprise, and then anger. Amidst a flurry of angry murmurs in the room, he rose and reached into his coat, producing a sheet of white paper. Then he shouted: "Wait a minute. I have a note here from my wife. It says, 'Keep your shirt on!'"

Everyone in the room burst into laughter, and the angry excitement died down, at least temporarily.[9]

Anger that is allowed to rage on eventually plays out in one of two ways: abuse—which may take the form of physical blows or emotional wounding—or estrangement. Both abuse and estrangement are painful situations, and reconciliation can be very difficult. The healing process is often a long one. How much better to channel the intense feelings of anger into positive, productive expenditures of energy, and whenever possible, to lighten the moment.

From the fruit of his mouth a man's stomach is filled; with the harvest from his lips he is satisfied. The tongue has the power of life and death, and those who love it will eat its fruit.

PROVERBS 18:20, 21 NIV

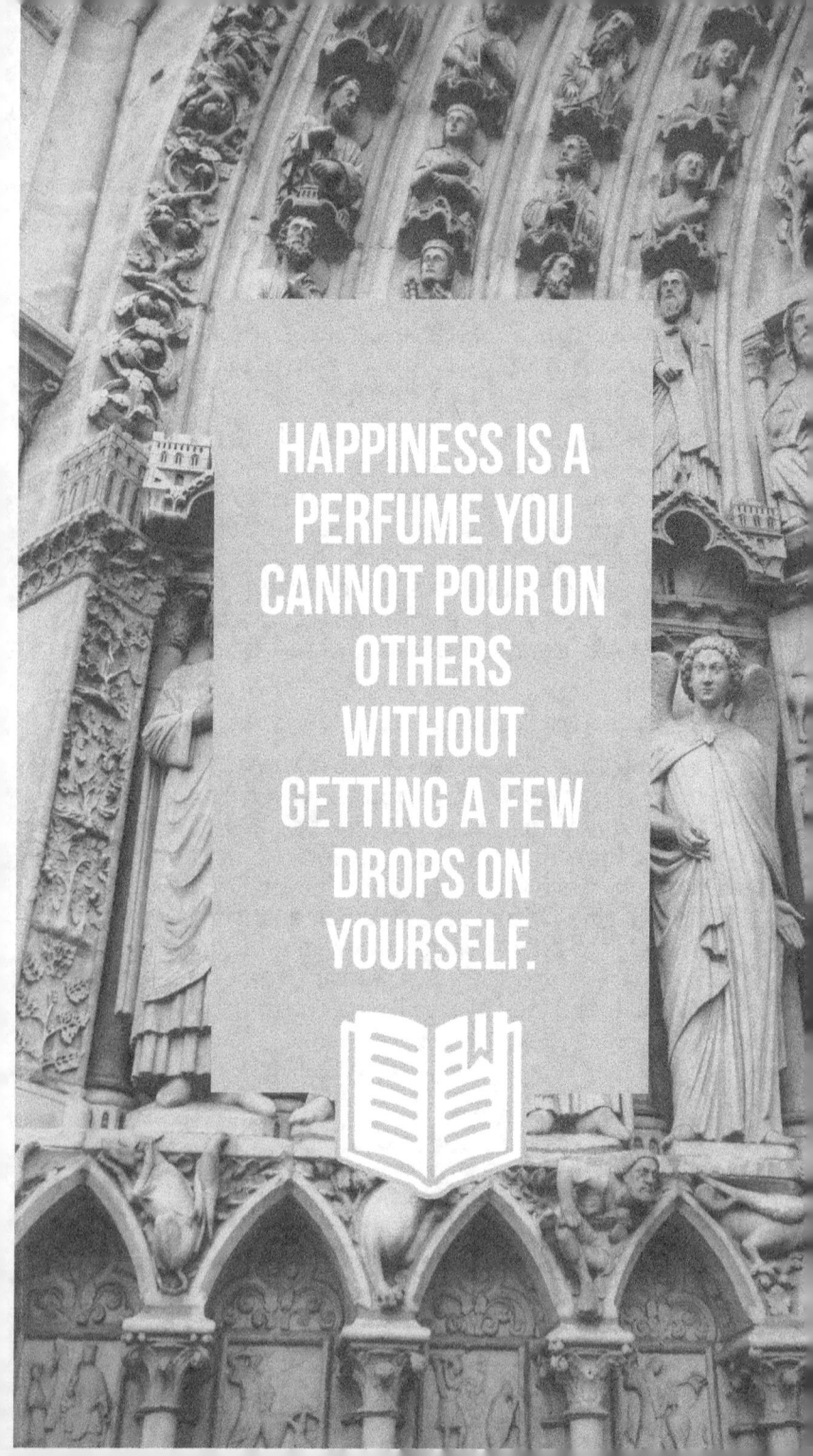

HAPPINESS IS A PERFUME YOU CANNOT POUR ON OTHERS WITHOUT GETTING A FEW DROPS ON YOURSELF.

Hyrum Smith has written, "When I was eight years old, living in the Hawaiian Islands, it appeared that Christmas was going to be pretty lean for our household. My parents . . . gathered us together . . . to explain to my siblings and me (there were seven of us) that there was not a great deal of money for Christmas. Each of us would have to select one gift that we really wanted, and that one gift would likely be the only one we would receive." Smith loved apples so he asked for a bushel of them.

His parents were astonished, but on Christmas morning they managed to present to him "the most wonderful bushel of apples I have ever seen." It was only years later that Smith realized that since apples don't grow in Hawaii, they had to be shipped in. He had asked for a very expensive present!

He recalls, "As soon as the rest of my family had opened their presents, I grabbed my bushel of apples and went out into the neighborhood to find all my friends. Within a few hours, I had given all of my apples away . . . I remember how wonderful it was to share my apples with all my friends . . . the fact that they were gone before sundown was not a problem for me." Out of that experience, Smith later came to an understanding of what he calls, "the abundance mentality."[10]

The more cheerfully we give to others, the more abundantly we receive.

"Happy are those who long to be just and good, for they shall be completely satisfied."

MATTHEW 5:6 TLB

WISDOM IS THE QUALITY THAT KEEPS YOU FROM GETTING INTO SITUATIONS WHERE YOU NEED IT.

One day, three rough-looking fellows on huge motorcycles pulled up to a highway cafe. Inside, they found only a waitress, the cook, and one truck driver—a little guy perched on a stool at the counter. The driver was quietly eating his lunch.

The motorcyclists, angry because they felt a trucker had cut them off several miles back, decided to take out their revenge on this innocent man. They grabbed his food away from him and mocked him, laughing in his face and calling him bad names. The truck driver said nothing. He simply got up, paid for his food, and walked out.

One of the three men, unhappy that they hadn't succeeded in provoking the little man into a fist fight, said to the waitress, "He sure wasn't much of a man, was he?"

The waitress replied, "I guess not." Then looking out the window, she added, "I guess he's not much of a truck driver either. He just ran over three motorcycles on his way out of the parking lot."[11]

The majority of the problems we have in life are actually of our own making—either through things we have said or done, or things we haven't said and haven't done. Now is always a good time to ask God for the wisdom to make choices that will keep us out of trouble in the future.

I would have you learn this great fact: that a life of doing right is the wisest life there is. If you live that kind of life, you'll not limp or stumble as you run.

PROVERBS 4:11, 12 TLB

RANK DOES NOT CONFER PRIVILEGE OR GIVE POWER. IT IMPOSES RESPONSIBILITY.

Sadhu Sundar Singh was born into an Indian family of high caste. When he became a Christian and told his parents of his decision to follow Christ, they said, "You have broken caste. You cannot live here any longer." They immediately banished him from their home.

It was the wet season and the rain was coming down hard as he left his home, clad in only his insubstantial Indian robes. He sat under a nearby tree all night, soaked to the skin. He said that he felt so radiantly happy, however, that he forgot any physical discomfort. He had the freedom to travel throughout the region telling the Gospel story.

He became known as the apostle of India. Once, he went into Tibet, where he was arrested, put into a pit, and branded with irons. He bore those scars the rest of his life. While speaking in England he said, "I am going back to do what I have done. I am quite aware of the cost." Some time after his return, he disappeared and appears to have suffered a martyr's death.[12]

Singh moved from "high caste" in India into a "servant's caste" for the Gospel. His position in Christ was not only marked by the privilege of eternal life, but by the responsibility to serve others and share Christ's love.

> "For everyone to whom much is given, of him shall much be required; and of him to whom men entrust much, they will require and demand all the more."
>
> LUKE 12:48 AMP

GOD HAS A
HISTORY OF
USING THE
INSIGNIFICANT
TO ACCOMPLISH
THE
IMPOSSIBLE.

In an upscale neighborhood of Chicago, a young married woman—popular, intelligent, wealthy—found herself overwhelmed by the headlines she read every day. Finally, she went to a neighbor and said, "Mary, you can laugh if you like or say no if you want, but would you consider meeting with me once a month, just the two of us, to pray for the world?" Her friend was startled but answered her seriously, "Let's make it once a week." And so these two women met together for weekly prayer. As the months went by, they invited others to join them and before long, they had a fully functioning prayer group.

One day one of the women asked, "I wonder if I might share something personal?" She told the group about certain marital difficulties she was having. Other women expressed similar problems, and that day, the group did what it could to help its own members. Their prayer focused on their own needs. It quickly became evident to these young women that they could not hope to reform the world unless they began with themselves. They invited their husbands to join the group and help them to combat the immorality that was the cause of so many of their personal problems. The results were so far-reaching that the entire community was changed![13]

Great oaks still grow from little acorns.

And Jesus looking upon them saith, "With men it is impossible, but not with God: for with God all things are possible."

MARK 10:27

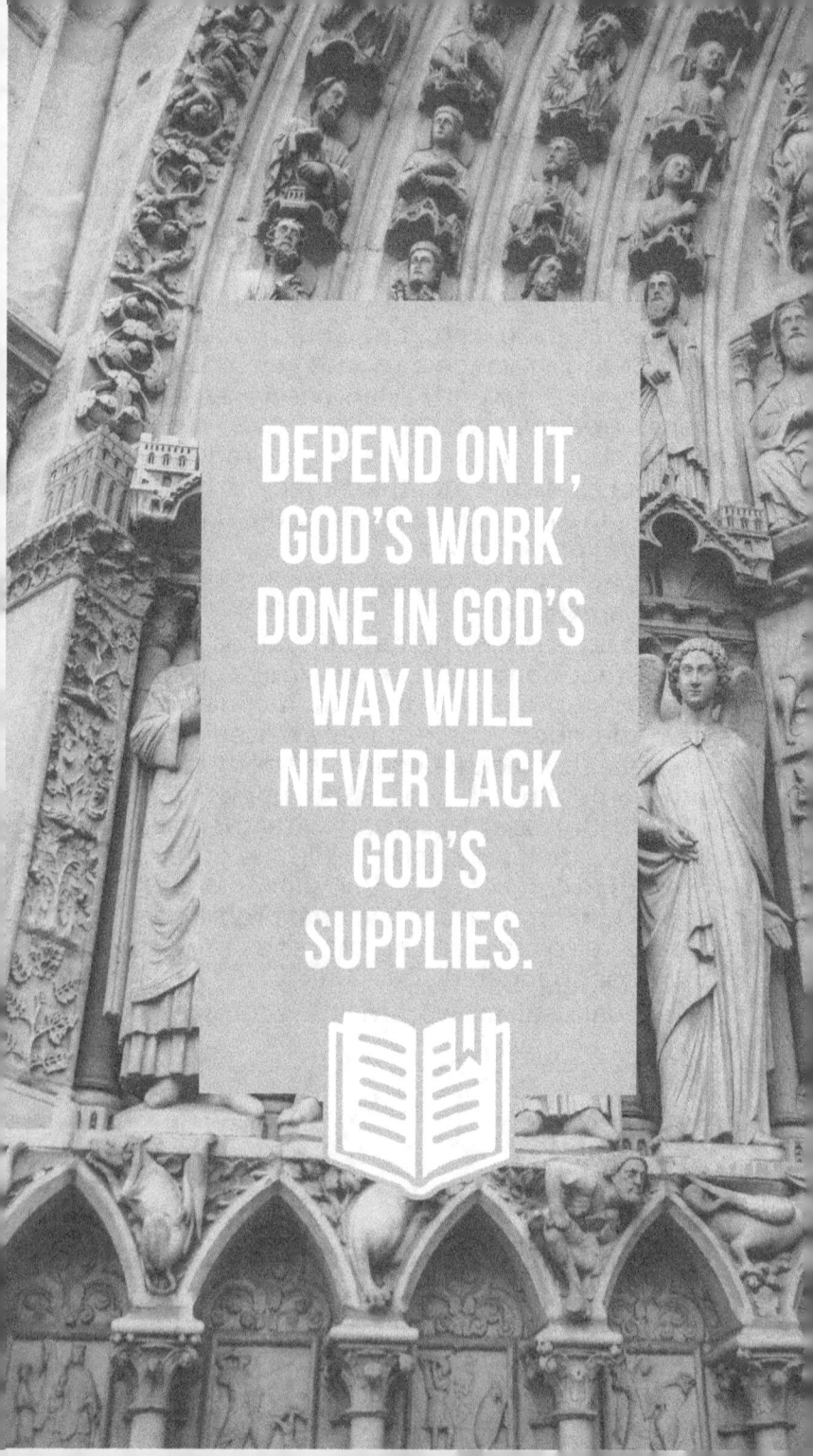

DEPEND ON IT, GOD'S WORK DONE IN GOD'S WAY WILL NEVER LACK GOD'S SUPPLIES.

A priest in a rural area asked one of his parishioners to serve as the parish's financial chairman. The man, who managed the largest grain elevator in the area, agreed based on two conditions: no report would be due for a year, and no one would ask any questions about the finances during the year. Although the second request seemed unorthodox, and would involve a great deal of trust, the priest and other key parishioners agreed. They valued the man's expertise and wisdom.

At the end of the year the man made his report. He had paid off the church debt of $200,000. He had redecorated the church, sent $1,000 to missions, and had $5,000 in the bank.

"How did you do all this?" the priest asked. He did have some understanding of what the weekly offerings had been. The congregation, the vast majority of whom were grain farmers, were equally shocked. The financial chairman answered quietly, "Well, you people all bring your grain to my elevator. As you did business with me, I simply withheld 10 percent and gave it to the church. You never missed it. But it sure added up."[14]

When we are generous toward God's work, we will usually find that what remains is more than sufficient to meet our own needs.

"If you are willing and obedient, you will eat the best from the land."

ISAIAH 1:19 NIV

IT'S NOT HOW
MANY HOURS
YOU PUT IN
BUT HOW
MUCH YOU PUT
INTO THE
HOURS.

One day, in a very busy factory, an intricate piece of machinery broke down. The company's best machinists were called in to diagnose the problem, but they couldn't come up with a solution.

Finally, they suggested a specialist be brought in. The master mechanic arrived, looked the apparatus over thoroughly, and then asked for the smallest hammer they had on hand. He then pecked on a critical area of the machine with the hammer, and said, "Now turn on the power. It ought to work." His small peck apparently released a mechanism that had jammed, and sure enough, the machine worked.

Later, when the specialist sent a bill for $100, the managers were astounded! One hundred dollars was an exorbitant fee for one small peck! They asked him to send them an itemized statement. He complied, but didn't reduce his fee. His statement read:

$1 for pecking
$99 for knowing where to peck[15]

A similar story is told about a young medical student who asked an experienced surgeon how long it would take to learn how to perform an appendectomy. The surgeon replied, "Three hours." Then he added, "And three years to learn what to do if anything goes wrong."

Put as much as you can into every hour. You'll have much more to draw upon later!

Whatever you do, work at it with all your heart, as working for the Lord, not for men . . . it is the Lord Christ you are serving.

COLOSSIANS 3:23,24 NIV

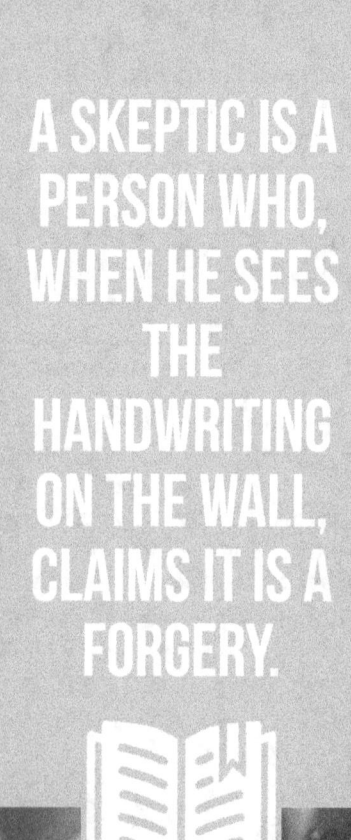

A SKEPTIC IS A PERSON WHO, WHEN HE SEES THE HANDWRITING ON THE WALL, CLAIMS IT IS A FORGERY.

G. Gordon Liddy, a White House aide during the Nixon administration, was a student of the German philosopher Nietzsche. Nietzsche taught that man's will was of supreme importance, not God's. A man with a will of iron, Liddy saw no need for God.

After serving a four-year prison term for his part in the Watergate scandal, Liddy renewed his friendship with some former FBI colleagues, who asked him to join their Bible study. He agreed, with one caveat: "Please do not try to convert me." Of course, things didn't work out as Liddy had anticipated. He had been willing to read the Bible as an historical document, but his friends' attitudes toward the Bible made him take a closer look.

He began to think about God. *If God is infinite and we're finite,* he thought, *how can we ever understand Him?* Liddy reasoned, *God will have to communicate with me.* Then he realized, *the Bible is God's communication.* Still, he argued, *we can never be worthy of God.* And again, he was hit by a thunderbolt: *God sent His Son to make us worthy* (by virtue of His crucifixion and resurrection), *and to keep the dialogue going between God and man.* Liddy suddenly perceived a need for God and he accepted Christ.[16]

God is surely alive. The question is: Is God alive in you today?

The fool hath said in his heart,
"There is no God."

PSALM 14:1

TWO THINGS
ARE BAD FOR
THE HEART—
RUNNING UP
STAIRS AND
RUNNING
DOWN PEOPLE.

n *Lessons from Mom*, Joan Aho Ryan writes about loyalty in friendship. She says, "We went to one of the local shopping malls recently where Mom ran into two women who live in her development ... They greeted her effusively. It was a brief exchange, during which she introduced me, and they were on their way. 'What phony baloney,' she said excitedly when they were well ahead of us. Since her remark came from nowhere, I asked her what she meant.

"With obvious disdain, she explained that she has sat under the canopy at her pool on several occasions with these two women and one of their friends, Sylvia. One day, she said, she sat nearby and heard the three of them talking about the wedding reception of Sylvia's daughter the week before. They raved about the food, the flowers, the elegant country club location, the beautiful bride ... Mom said Sylvia was obviously beaming with pride.

"'Well, then Sylvia left, and you should have heard them,' Mom said ... 'I couldn't believe friends could be that two-faced. They ripped her apart, talking about how cheap she was, her homely son-in-law, the music they couldn't dance to. It was awful. And they call themselves friends,' she clucked. 'Who needs friends like that?'"[17]

Speaking well of others is not only a good way to acquire friends, but to keep them.

Let no corrupt communication proceed out of your mouth, but that which is good to the use of edifying, that it may minister grace unto the hearers.

EPHESIANS 4:29

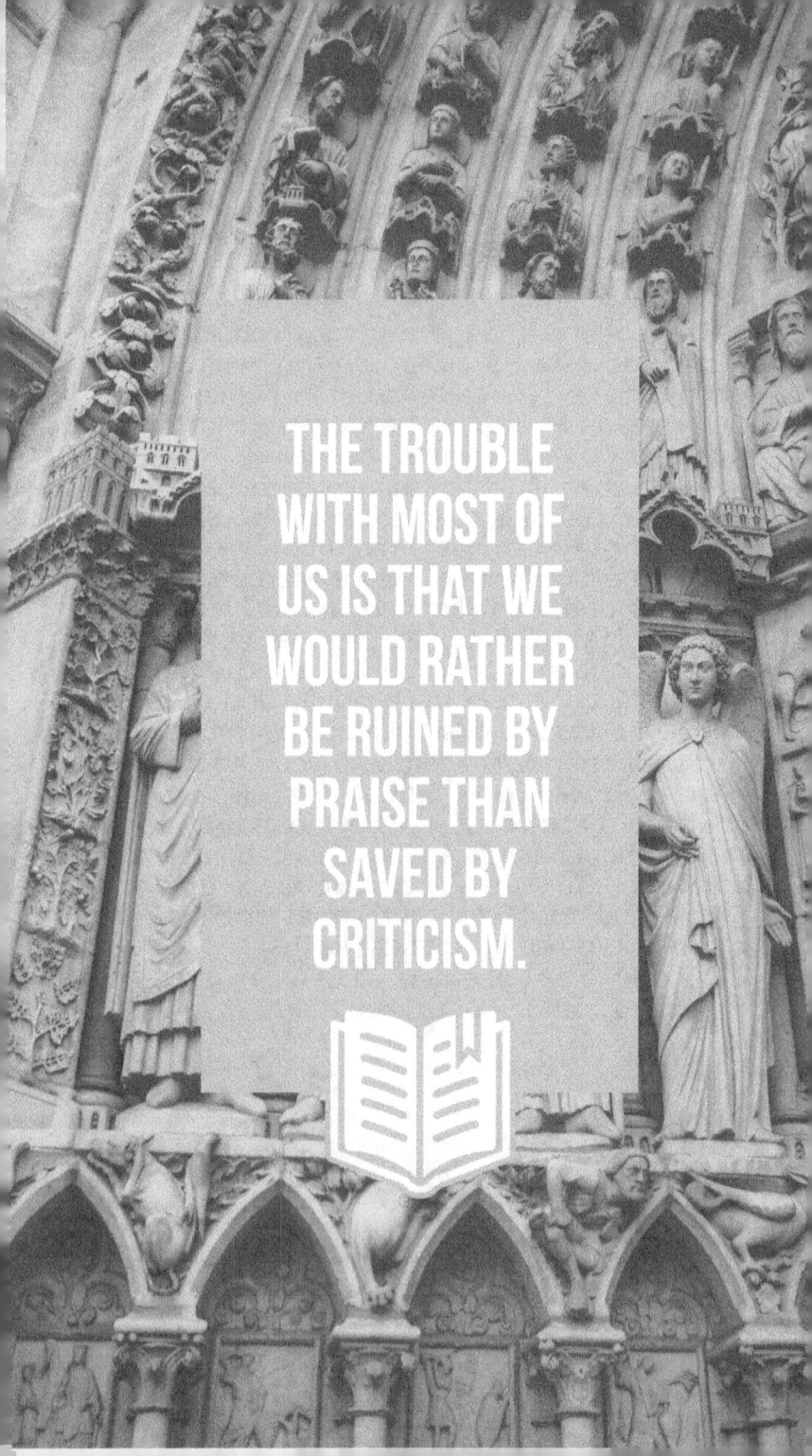

THE TROUBLE
WITH MOST OF
US IS THAT WE
WOULD RATHER
BE RUINED BY
PRAISE THAN
SAVED BY
CRITICISM.

The story is told of two Christian men who once had a "falling out." One heard a rumor that the other was speaking against him, so he went to him and said, "Will you be kind enough to tell my faults to my face, that I may profit by your Christian candor and try to get rid of them?" The other man replied, "Yes, I will."

They then went aside from the crowd and the first man said, "Before you commence telling what you think wrong in me, will you kneel with me and pray, that my eyes may be opened to see my faults as you cite them? You lead in prayer."

The second man prayed that God would open the eyes of his friend and when he was finished, the first man said, "Now, please proceed with your complaints."

The second man said, "After praying over it, it looks so little that it is not worth talking about. The truth is I have been serving the devil myself, and have need that you pray for me, and forgive me the wrong I have done you."[18]

Two things are admirable: to speak the truth to another person with love, and with love to seek the truth from one who will be honest with you. In speaking the truth, we often hear the very truth we need to hear, from our own lips. In seeking the truth, we often gain a friend.

If you profit from constructive criticism you will be elected to the wise men's hall of fame. But to reject criticism is to harm yourself and your own best interests.

PROVERBS 15:31,32 TLB

PEOPLE MAY
DOUBT WHAT
YOU SAY, BUT
THEY WILL
ALWAYS
BELIEVE WHAT
YOU DO.

A minister was scheduled to speak at an all-day conference. He failed to set his alarm, however, and he overslept. In his haste to make up for lost time, he cut himself while shaving. Then, he discovered his shirt was not ironed and scorched it because the iron was too hot. To make matters worse, as he ran out to his car he noticed that he had a flat tire.

Disgusted and distraught, by the time he finished changing the tire he was an hour behind schedule. Nevertheless, the minister felt encouraged when he was finally "under way." He figured that if he hurried, he might be only a few minutes late for the first session. He raced through town, failing to notice a stop sign along the way. As he rushed through it, he caught a glimpse of a policeman, who sure enough, stopped him.

Jumping out of his car, the agitated minister said sharply, "Go ahead and give me a ticket. Everything else has gone wrong today." The policeman quietly responded, "I used to have days like that before I became a Christian."[19]

Your Christian witness lies far more in your everyday lifestyle than in what you have to say about your Christianity.

"... for the tree is known and recognized and judged by its fruit."

MATTHEW 12:33 AMP

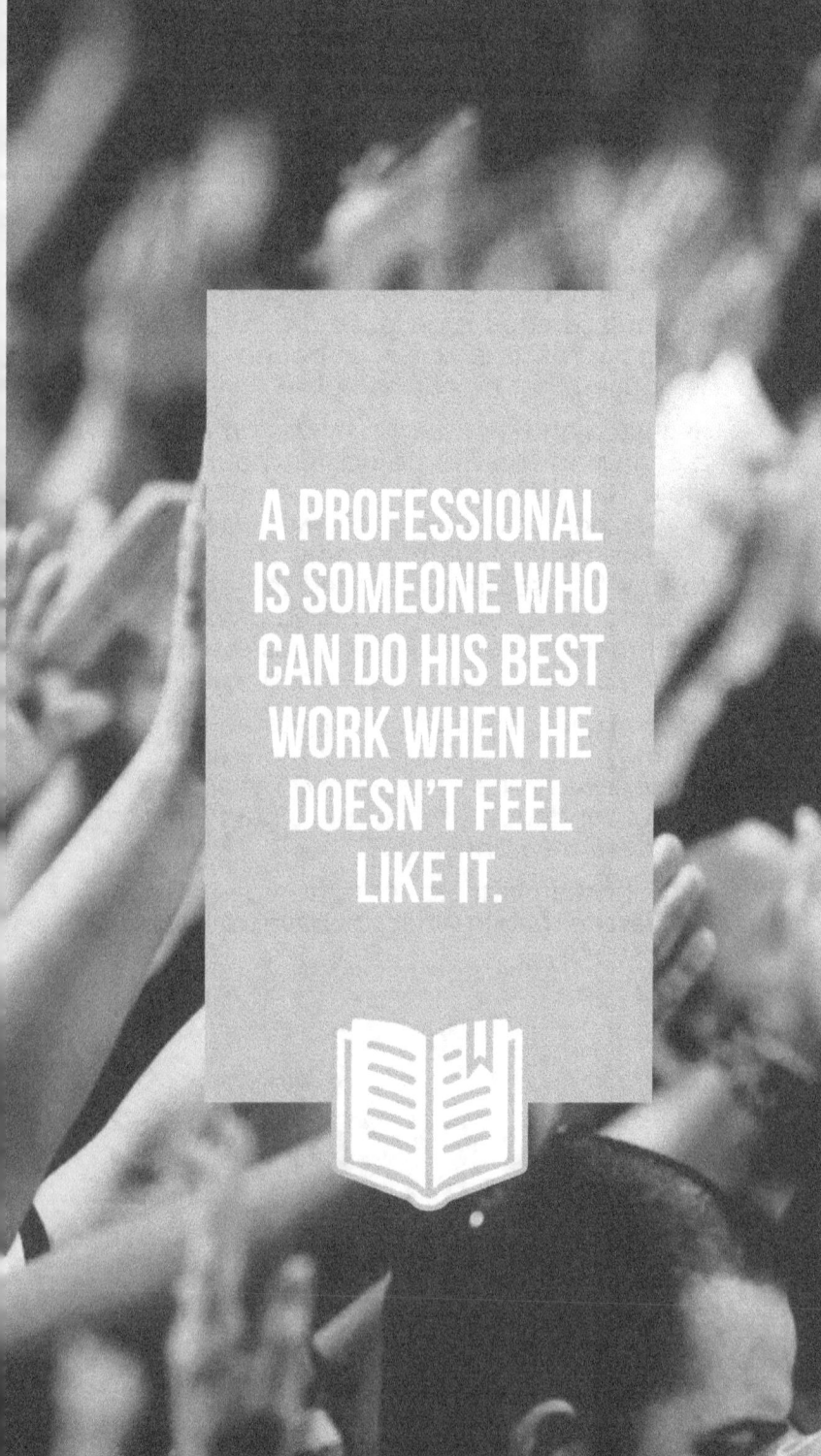

A PROFESSIONAL IS SOMEONE WHO CAN DO HIS BEST WORK WHEN HE DOESN'T FEEL LIKE IT.

A husband and wife rose early one Sunday morning. They had breakfast, and then the wife retired to the bedroom to dress for church. As the time was approaching when they needed to leave for the morning service, she noticed that her husband hadn't made any move toward getting dressed. She asked, "Why aren't you getting dressed for church?"

He said, "'Cause I don't want to go."

She asked, "Do you have any good reasons?"

He said, "Yes, I have three good reasons."

"And they are?" she asked.

"First, the congregation is cold. Second, no one likes me. And third, I just don't want to go this morning."

The wife replied with wisdom, "Well, honey, I have three reasons why you should go."

"Convince me," he said.

"First, the congregation is warm. Second, there are a few people there who like you. And third, you're the pastor. So get dressed!"[20]

Nobody likes doing what is right and good all the time. We each have moments when we would rather give a halfhearted effort or yield to temptation. The mark of professionalism, however, is in facing down what you don't want to do by doing it anyway.

To win the contest you must deny yourselves many things that would keep you from doing your best.

1 CORINTHIANS 9:25 TLB

FOR PEACE OF
MIND,
RESIGN AS
GENERAL
MANAGER OF
THE UNIVERSE.

Someone once studied the inaugural speeches of—United States presidents. Special focus was placed upon presidents who had been reelected to a second term. One of the purposes of the study was to determine how many times the word "I" appeared.

Washington's first inaugural address contained 1,300 words and twenty "I's." His second inaugural speech was much shorter.

Lincoln's first inaugural speech had 3,588 words, with forty-three "I's." His second had only 588 words and a solitary "I."

In the Bible, Romans 7 is a chapter filled with struggle, conflict, and failure. It contains thirty-two "I's" and sixteen "me's and my's,"—forty-eight personal pronouns in all. In chapter eight, which tells of victory, triumph, and peace, "I" and "me" are hardly mentioned.[21]

One of the great lessons of experience is when we learn that we are not the prime motivator or catalyst of the success we experience in life. While we may be the engineer of our own failures more often than we care to admit, we rarely reach the heights of success on our own. We always have the help of others in reaching the top—regardless of our field or endeavor—and ultimately, we are enabled by God. We accomplish only what He enables us to.

Cease striving and know that I am God.

PSALM 46:10 NASB

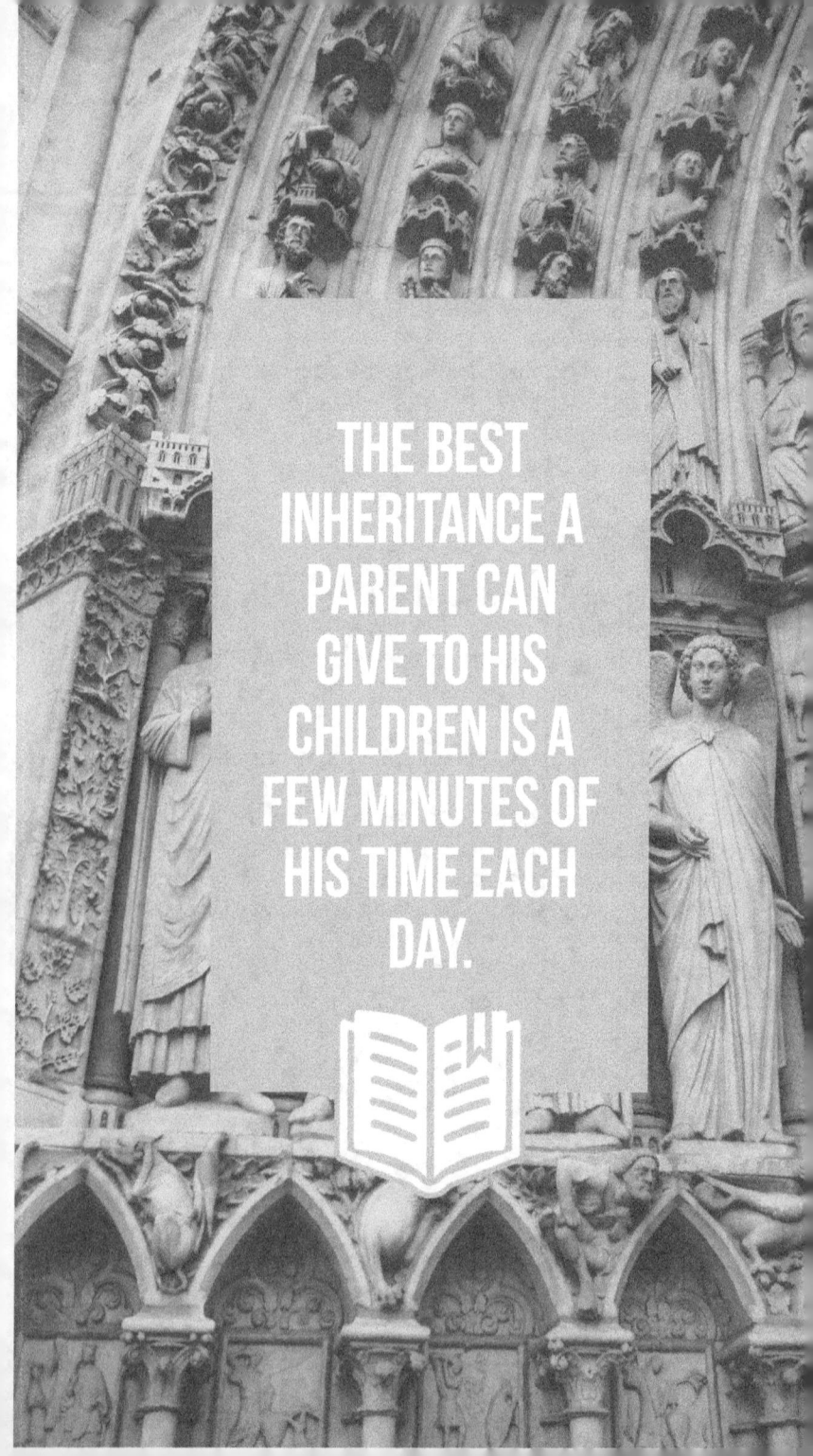

THE BEST
INHERITANCE A
PARENT CAN
GIVE TO HIS
CHILDREN IS A
FEW MINUTES OF
HIS TIME EACH
DAY.

n *From Bad Beginnings to Happy Endings*, Ed Young writes, "Several years ago I was invited to the White House to meet with a few key religious leaders and the President of the United States. Now that was a pretty good offer, wasn't it? It was the first invitation from a president this old country boy from Mississippi had ever received. I'd been out of town during the first part of the week and between flights I called home to check in. When I did, I learned that my son Ben's basketball game originally scheduled for midweek had been rescheduled for the end of the week—and I'd missed one game already!

"The question was one of simple priority: 'What's the most important thing to me?' Since the government had been running pretty well without me for a number of years, I called the White House and said, 'Ed Young won't be coming.' (They recovered from this news beautifully.) Instead I went to the game and had the fun of seeing my son shoot the winning basket."[22]

The management of our time is the single most important area of life for the application of our values and the manifestation of our priorities. What are you spending your time on today? How much time are you giving to those things or people that matter most to you?

Be very careful, then, how you live—not as unwise but as wise, making the most of every opportunity.

EPHESIANS 5:15, 16 NIV

NO ONE IS
USELESS IN
THIS WORLD
WHO LIGHTENS
THE BURDEN
OF ANYONE
ELSE.

Best-selling author Leo Buscaglia was the youngest son of a very large Italian immigrant family. He grew up speaking Italian at home, learning English as a second language. As a boy, he preferred opera to popular music, and he knew Italian fairy tales rather than the traditional English ones read by his neighbors. His family's home was marked by joyous moments, passionate beliefs, and deep family ties.

However, his school psychologist saw him differently. He considered Buscaglia's English language skills to be very low, and his view of the world radically unrealistic. The psychologist classified him as mentally deficient, "retarded," and recommended that he be placed in a special class.

In the special class, Buscaglia met Miss Hunt, a caring, warm teacher who paid little attention to the label placed upon him. She saw him, and the other students in her class, as rich in potential. She conveyed a love of learning to all her students.

Buscaglia soon blossomed, and after several months, Miss Hunt insisted that he be re-tested. The result was his placement in a regular classroom. Miss Hunt's door remained open to Buscaglia, and she continued to encourage him and convince him that he had a wonderful life ahead.[23]

What might you do today to help someone who has been "written off" by others?

Now we who are strong ought to bear the weaknesses of those without strength and not just please ourselves. Let each of us please his neighbor for his good, to his edification.

ROMANS 15:1,2 NASB

ANGER IS A
STONE
THROWN AT A
WASP'S
NEST.

The story is told of two farmers who lived next to each other, with nothing but a river dividing their property. One day when the corn was ripe, the cows of one neighbor got out of their pasture and crossed the river into the other farmer's waving field of corn. They trampled and ruined about half an acre of the crop. The farmer who owned the damaged corn crop rounded up the cattle and put them in his barn. He made his neighbor pay dearly for every ear of corn the cows had destroyed before he would return them to him.

That fall, the hogs of the man whose com had been eaten got out and crossed the river into the potato patch of the neighbor. They obliterated it. The hog owner saw his hogs and the damage they were doing, so he got his gun and hid himself. He vowed that if his neighbor harmed his hogs, he would shoot him. When he saw that his neighbor had no intention of hurting the hogs, he was surprised. He said to him, "You have something I do not have. What is it?" The neighbor replied, "I am a Christian."

That night the unregenerate man and his wife crossed the river and visited their neighbors. Both were converted before they left his home.[24]

Do not be quick in spirit to be angry or vexed, for anger and vexation lodge in the bosom of fools.

ECCLESIASTES 7:9 AMP

WISDOM IS THE WEALTH OF THE WISE.

Many years ago in South Africa, a man sold his farm so that he might spend his days in search of diamonds. He was consumed with dreams of becoming wealthy. When he had finally exhausted his resources and his health, and was no closer to his fortune than the day he sold his farm, he threw himself into a river and drowned.

One day, the man who had bought his farm spotted an unusual-looking stone in a creek bed. He placed it on his fireplace mantle as a conversation piece. A visitor noticed the stone and examined it closely. He then stated his suspicion that the stone was actually a diamond. The farmer, very discreetly, had the stone analyzed, and sure enough, it was one of the largest and finest diamonds ever found.

Still operating under great secrecy, the farmer searched his stream, gathering similar stones. They were all diamonds. In fact, his farm was covered with diamonds just waiting to be picked up! The farm the diamond-seeker had sold turned out to be one of the richest diamond deposits in the world.[25]

The lessons of wisdom can often be learned in the relationships and experiences we encounter every day. Ask God to reveal to you what you need to know in order to live the life He desires for you to live. The resources you need are probably right there in front of you.

For the value of wisdom is far above rubies; nothing can be compared with it.

PROVERBS 8:11 TLB

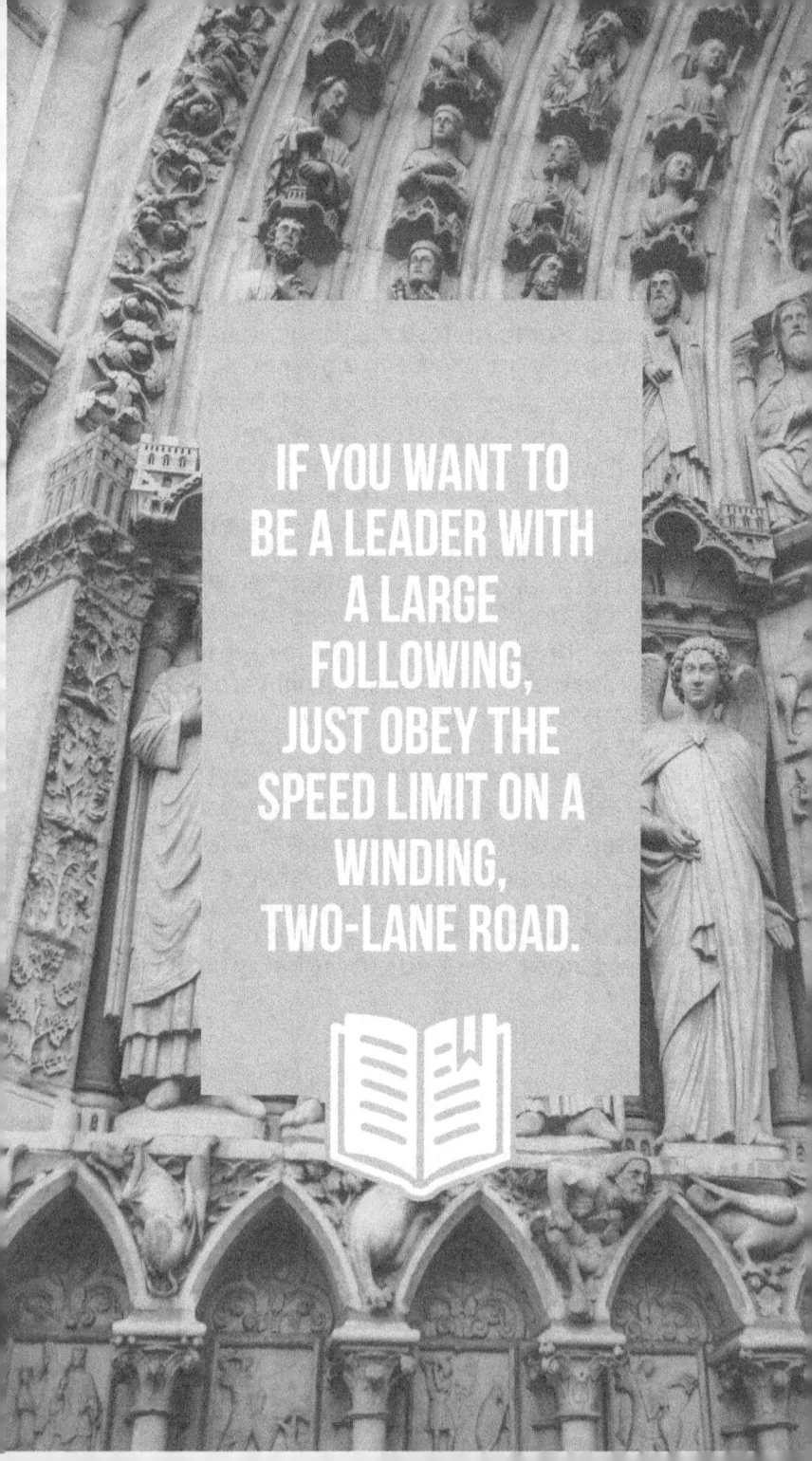

In *Values from the Heartland*, Bettie Youngs writes about her father, who got his start in farming on a rented farm near Vincent, Iowa. In need of financial backing to expand his operation, he turned to Art Swasand at the Farmer's Savings Bank. Art did business the old-fashioned way: a client's character was an important part of the deal.

Art had a reputation for going the extra mile and doing whatever it took to develop and maintain a successful working relationship. When her father's tractor broke down one day, Art drove out to visit him. Once he understood what was needed to get the tractor running again, Art financed the parts on the spot.

Says Youngs, "Over the years, these two men financed and paid off machinery, created financial security, purchased land . . . and raised their families. Without fanfare, they became prosperous men doing what they each loved best, with integrity." Youngs' father said of Art after his death, "In more ways than one he was a father, a brother, a confidant, a friend. He was my ideal of a man."[26]

The way you travel through life is the greatest legacy you can leave to those who follow you. In living a life of upright values and strong faith, you are not only making a path through life, you are leading the way to Heaven.

Everyone has heard about your obedience, so I am full of joy over you; but I want you to be wise about what is good, and innocent about what is evil.

ROMANS 16:19 NIV

URGENT THINGS
ARE SELDOM
IMPORTANT.
IMPORTANT
THINGS ARE
SELDOM
URGENT.

A man in Vermont once was invited to join a friend of his for a ride through the timberland in their area. His friend, a lumberjack, drove him up Mt. Cushman in a jeep. Near the top of the mountain, he noticed some six-inch deciduous seedlings that had obviously been planted by someone.

The man asked his friend when the seedlings would be ready to harvest for lumber and the lumberjack replied, "In the year 2015." Noting that this was some sixty years into the future and that his friend was well into middle age, he asked his friend why he had planted the trees, since he would never see the harvest.

He replied, "Because my grandfather planted some on the other side of the mountain for me."[27]

Building for a successful future always requires:

F — *faith that God will help you in your endeavor.*
U — *unction to get started and stay motivated.*
T — *thoughtful planning.*
U — *undying persistence.*
R — *reliance upon help from others.*
E — *endurance through tough times.*

When we focus on God's plan for the future, we make the right decisions today.

Every prudent man dealeth with knowledge.

PROVERBS 13:16

KINDNESS IS A LANGUAGE WHICH THE DEAF CAN HEAR AND THE BLIND CAN SEE.

Laura Ingalls Wilder writes in *Little House in the Ozarks*, "We had a 'working' in our neighborhood this winter. That is a blessed, old-fashioned way of helping out a neighbor. While the winter was warm, still it had been much too cold to be without firewood; and this neighbor, badly crippled with rheumatism, was not able to get up his winter's wood. With what little wood he could manage to chop, the family scarcely kept comfortable. So the men of the neighborhood gathered together one morning and dropped in on him. With cross-cut saws and axes, they took possession of his wood lot. At noon a wood saw was brought in, and it sawed briskly all the afternoon. By night there was enough wood ready for the stove to last the rest of the winter.

"The women did their part, too. All morning they kept arriving with well-filled baskets, and at noon a long table was filled with a country neighborhood dinner . . . When the dishes were washed, they sewed, knit, crocheted, and talked for the rest of the afternoon. It was a regular old-fashioned good time, and we all went home with the feeling expressed by a newcomer when he said, 'Don't you know I'm proud to live in a neighborhood like this.'"[28]

Kindness is a universal language understood by all.

For his merciful kindness is great toward us: and the truth of the Lord endureth for ever. Praise ye the Lord.

PSALM 117:2

PEOPLE
WILL BE MORE
IMPRESSED
BY THE DEPTH
OF YOUR
CONVICTION
THAN THE HEIGHT
OF YOUR LOGIC.

Beth Raby once competed in a high school vocal competition in which the songs were to be sung in a foreign language. She had four weeks in which to prepare, but since she had a great deal going on in her life at the time, she didn't prepare as well as she might have. When the time came for her to perform for the judges, she couldn't remember some of the German words in her song. She threw in every German word she could think of! As a result, she did not receive her usual high marks. She felt awful.

On the way home, her teacher said to the group of students, "Don't worry. You did your best." That was all he expected. When they stopped to have lunch, however, Beth remained on the bus, where she burst into tears. She knew that she had not given her best. As she sobbed with her head down, she felt a hand on her back and looked up to see her teacher. He had big tears in his eyes, too.

Those tears, far more than any words spoken, brought healing to her heart. While she knew by his words he believed she could do better in the future, she knew by his touch that he would be there to help her. More than any other single thing, that touch helped Beth to become a compassionate teacher herself.[29]

My son, forget not my law; but let thine heart keep my commandments . . . So shalt thou find favour and good understanding in the sight of God and man.

PROVERBS 3:1,4

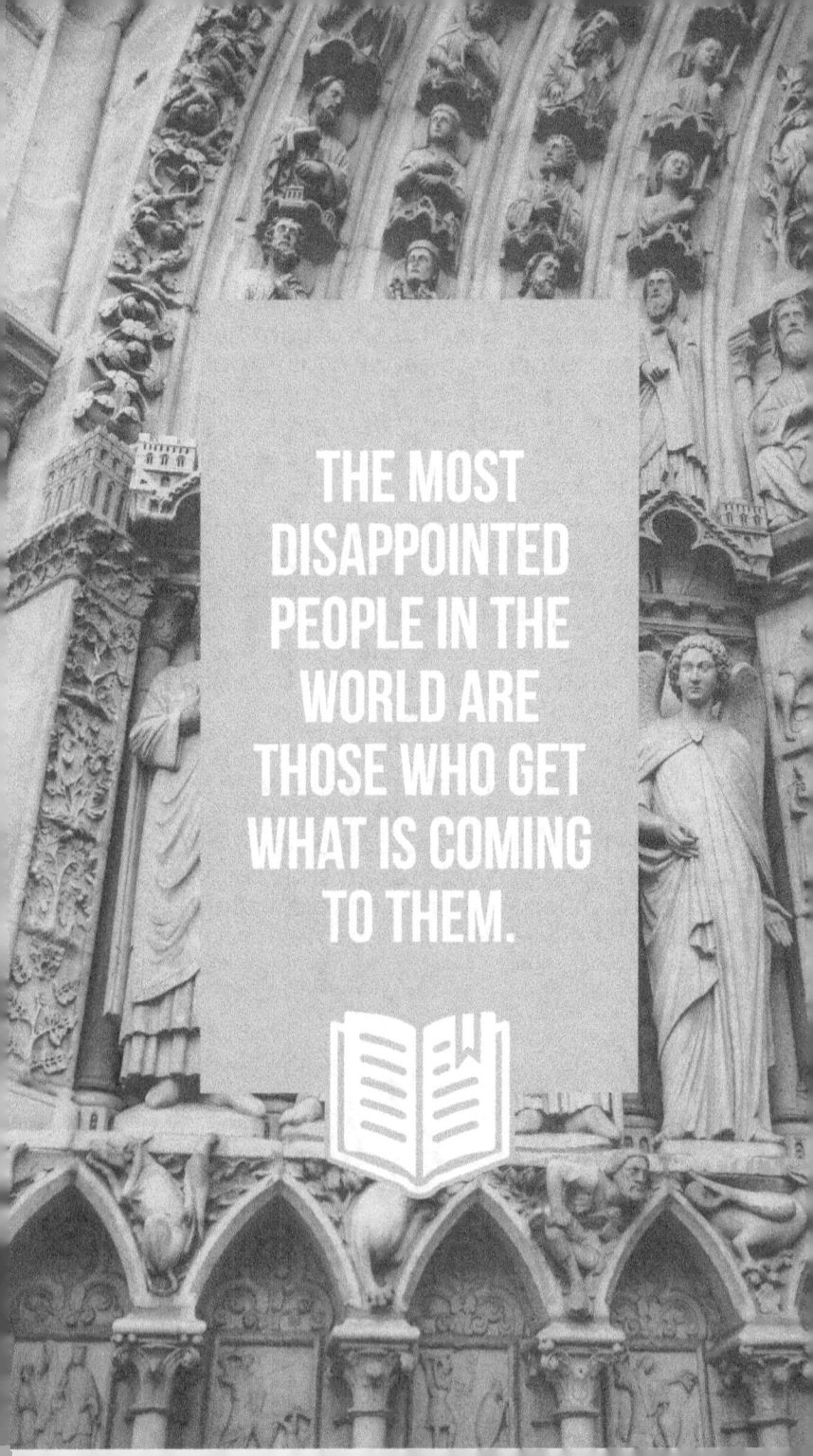

THE MOST
DISAPPOINTED
PEOPLE IN THE
WORLD ARE
THOSE WHO GET
WHAT IS COMING
TO THEM.

Many years ago when Egyptian troops conquered Nubia, a regiment of soldiers was crossing the Nubian desert with an Arab guide.

Recognizing that they had limited water and suffering from great thirst, the soldiers were deceived by the appearance of a beautiful lake on the horizon. They insisted that their guide take them to its banks. The guide, who knew the desert well, knew that what they saw was just a mirage. In vain, he told the men that the lake was not real. He refused to lose precious time by wandering from the designated course.

Angry words led to blows and in the end, the soldiers killed the guide. As they moved toward the lake, it receded into the distance. Finally, they recognized their delusion—the lake was only burning sand. Raging thirst and horrible despair engulfed the soldiers. Without their guide, the pathless desert was a mystery. They were lost and without water. Not one of them survived.[30]

Be sure that what you seek today is not only within the realm of reality, but even more importantly, that it is part of God's plan for your life. Any other goal is likely to be unworthy of pursuit, and may even be deadly.

A man's own folly ruins his life, yet his heart rages against the Lord.

PROVERBS 19:3 NIV

LIFE AFFORDS NO GREATER RESPONSIBILITY, NO GREATER PRIVILEGE, THAN THE RAISING OF THE NEXT GENERATION.

A parable has been told about a young mother who asked her guide in life, "Is the way long?" The guide said, "Yes, and hard. You will be old before you reach the end of it, but the end will be better than the beginning." The young mother was happy at that news but couldn't imagine any time being better than the days when she played with her children, gathered flowers for them, and bathed with them in clear streams.

Then night came, and with it a storm. Her children shook with fear and cold and their mother drew them close. They said, "We are not afraid, for you are near." The mother said, "This is better than the brightness of day; I have taught my children courage."

The next day, the mother and her children climbed a steep hill. When they reached the top, the children said, "We could not have done it without you, Mother." She said, "This is a better day than the last, for my children have learned fortitude. I have given them strength."

The next day came strange clouds of darkness — of war, hate, and evil. The children groped and stumbled but their mother said, "Lift your eyes to the Light." That night she said, "This is the best day of all, for I have shown my children God."

And so it was, each day better than the one before, until she died and began her most glorious day of all.[31]

> "Teach them [God's commandments] to your children, talking about them when you sit at home and when you walk along the road, when you lie down and when you get up . . . so that your days and the days of your children may be many."
>
> DEUTERONOMY 11:19, 21 NIV

COMPROMISE MAKES A GOOD UMBRELLA BUT A POOR ROOF; IT IS A TEMPORARY EXPEDIENT.

Thirty years ago, Sandy Koufax—a Jewish pitcher for the Los Angeles Dodgers—announced that he wouldn't play on the holiest day of his year, Yom Kippur. Koufax's employer pointed out that it was the first game of the 1965 World Series. Couldn't he pitch just a little? "No," Koufax said. But, he pitched a shutout in games five and seven, and the Dodgers won the series 4-3.

In 1996, Eli Herring, a 340-pound offensive tackle, who sported a 3.5 grade-point average, was expected to be the top senior offensive tackle in the pro draft. However, he turned down a possible multimillion-dollar deal with the Oakland Raiders because he wouldn't play on his holy day, Sunday.

Unfortunately, most of the Raiders games were scheduled for Sundays. Herring could either sign up with the NFL and enjoy a very prosperous life, or teach math for $20,000 a year, keep the Sabbath, and enjoy a very honorable life. He chose honor and conviction over riches.[32]

An old country-gospel song states the conviction underlying both men's decisions: "You can't be a beacon if your light don't shine."

A good mm is guided by his honesty; the evil man is destroyed by his dishonesty.

PROVERBS 11:3 TLB

PEOPLE WHO
FLY INTO A
RAGE ALWAYS
MAKE A BAD
LANDING.

The great maestro, Toscanini, was as well-known for his ferocious temper as he was for his outstanding musicianship. When members of his orchestra played badly, he often picked up whatever was within reach and hurled it to the floor in disgust. During one rehearsal someone misplayed a flat note, causing the genius to grab his valuable watch and smash it. The watch was broken beyond repair.

Shortly afterward, Toscanini received a luxurious velvet-lined box from his devoted musicians. The box contained two watches—one a beautiful gold timepiece, the other a cheap watch. On the back of the cheap watch was inscribed the words, "For rehearsals only."

While Toscanini's temper affected material things, Homer's was quite different. Legend has it that Homer encountered a group of boys on their way home from a fishing trip. When he asked them about their luck, they replied, "What we caught we threw away; what we didn't catch, we have." The boys were referring to fleas, and their bites, not to fish. Homer, however, could not guess their riddle and became so enraged that he killed himself.[33]

Anger rarely has a positive outcome, in your own life or in the lives of those around you. Learn how to diffuse it!

The discretion of a man deferreth his anger; and it is his glory to pass over a transgression.

PROVERBS 19:11

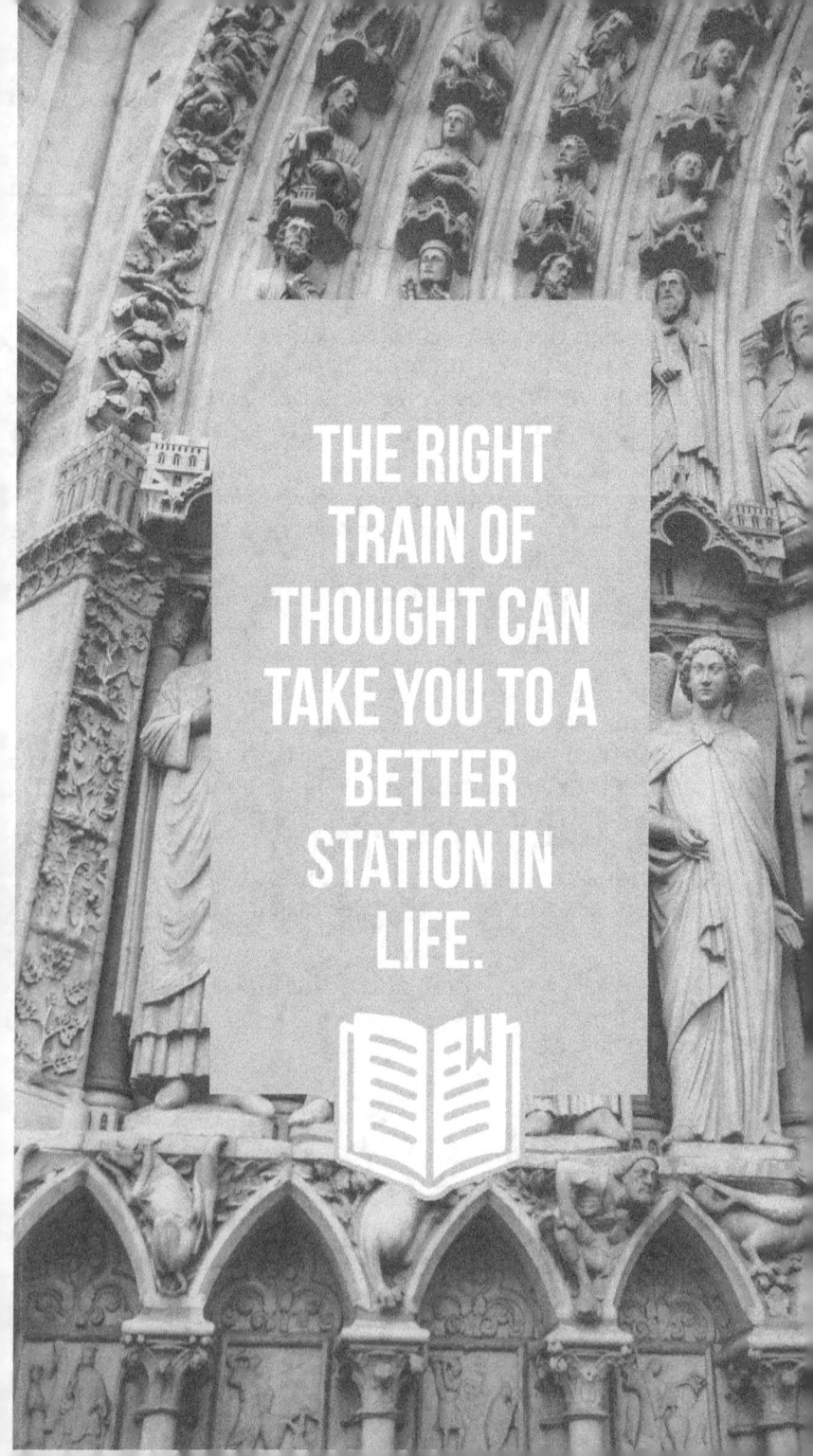

THE RIGHT
TRAIN OF
THOUGHT CAN
TAKE YOU TO A
BETTER
STATION IN
LIFE.

E dmond once vowed that he and his family would never be homeless. But, a short time later, he lost his job, and then fire destroyed their home. Suddenly, they were homeless. Their only option was a shelter.

At the end of the first day there, Edmond's prayer was, "Lord, get me out of here." His attitude was extremely negative. In his opinion, the shelter's rules were humiliating. Residents had to be escorted across the street to the mission hall for their meals. They had to attend a church that helped support the shelter. When residents found work, they were expected to put 70 percent of their paycheck in a savings fund toward the day when they could move out of the shelter.

After pouring out all his complaints to the shelter's director, Edmond had a restless night. He realized that he had been focusing all his attention on getting out, rather than on what he might do to make things easier for his family. That night, he changed his attitude. He started by taking a glass of water to a coughing man in the next room.

Nine months later, Edmond and his family had a home again. But he didn't forget what he had learned. He still visits the shelter, saying, "Wherever you are, God is there too." Attitude, not circumstances, made the real difference in his life.[34]

For as he thinks within himself, so he is.

PROVERBS 23:7 NASB

LIFE WAS A LOT SIMPLER WHEN WE HONORED FATHER AND MOTHER RATHER THAN ALL THE MAJOR CREDIT CARDS.

Leonard Pitts, Jr., has described the feeling he had when business took him to Natchez, Mississippi, where his mother was born and raised. Driving the streets of the town, he recalled how he had dreamed of the riches he had once hoped to give his mother. He said, "The costliest gift I ever gave [her] was a plane ticket. Actually, my sisters and brother and I all chipped in on that . . ."

"The ticket was a gift for what was to be her final birthday before cancer won its years-long battle. It seemed woefully inadequate in light of what she had given us: spirit riches in the shadow of poverty; security on the edge of apprehension; a home in a city jungle. Sick from heart disease and hypertension, abused by a husband who'd sold his soul to the bottle, she gave us ourselves. She made us women and men. What's a plane ticket compared with that?"

Pitts had all but forgotten the gift until he stopped at the home of his mother's lifelong friend, Isabel. She told him that his mother had said, "My life has been really rough. But if I didn't have my children, I don't know what I'd have done. My children sent me home for my birthday. I'd been wanting to come home one more time." Pitts reflected, "I had always wondered if she knew how grateful we were . . . She knew."[35]

Does your mother know?

Children, obey your parents in the Lord, for this is right. "Honor your father and mother"— which is the first commandment with a promise—"that it may go well with you and that you may enjoy long life on the earth"

EPHESIANS 6:1-3 NIV

SMART PEOPLE
SPEAK FROM
EXPERIENCE—
SMARTER
PEOPLE FROM
EXPERIENCE,
DON'T SPEAK.

An early American evangelist once generalized that all infidels were fools. Furthermore, he said he could prove his statement to be true for any given case within ten minutes.

A man in the audience stood up and proclaimed himself an infidel, but no fool.

The preacher looked him over and said, "So you are an infidel?"

"Certainly, sir, I deny that there is anything at all in religion."

"Nothing at all in religion? Are you willing to go on record as saying that?"

"Go on record?" the infidel replied. "Why, I have been writing and lecturing against religion for twenty years."

The evangelist glanced at his watch and said, "Well, I said I could prove an infidel a fool in ten minutes, and I still have seven minutes left. I'll leave it to the audience to decide if a man isn't a fool to write and lecture for twenty years against a thing that supposedly has nothing whatever in it!"[36]

Before you speak your mind, make certain that there's something in your mind worth speaking.

He who restrains his lips is wise.

PROVERBS 10:19 NASB

AN ATHEIST IS
A MAN WHO
HAS NO
INVISIBLE
MEANS OF
SUPPORT.

For years, an atheist in a Greek village envied the serenity of a Christian friend. Finally, he asked his friend if he thought God would give him the same peace of mind. The Christian said, "Yes, I believe so, if you get to know Him."

The atheist asked, "But where can I meet this God?" The Christian said that he customarily went out several miles beyond the village and there met and talked with God.

The next morning the atheist walked out away from the village until he stood before a mountain. He cried, "Lord God Almighty, show me the kind of being You are!" He received no answer although he cried out several times.

A few days later, he said to his Christian friend, "There is no God! I stood before the mountain day after day and called out to your God but there was no answer. I asked Him to tell me the kind of being He is."

The Christian replied, "Well, my friend, when I go out there, I tell God the kind of person I am. I confess I am sinful and cannot exist apart from Him. Then God appears to me and I understand Him better."

The atheist decided to try that approach and fell before the mountain, saying, "Lord, I am a sinful man. Forgive me." When he looked up, the mountain was gone. It had been only a shadow of himself, and once he was out of the way, he could see the Lord.[37]

Is there a mountain standing between you and God?

The fool hath said in his heart, "There is no God."

PSALM 53:1

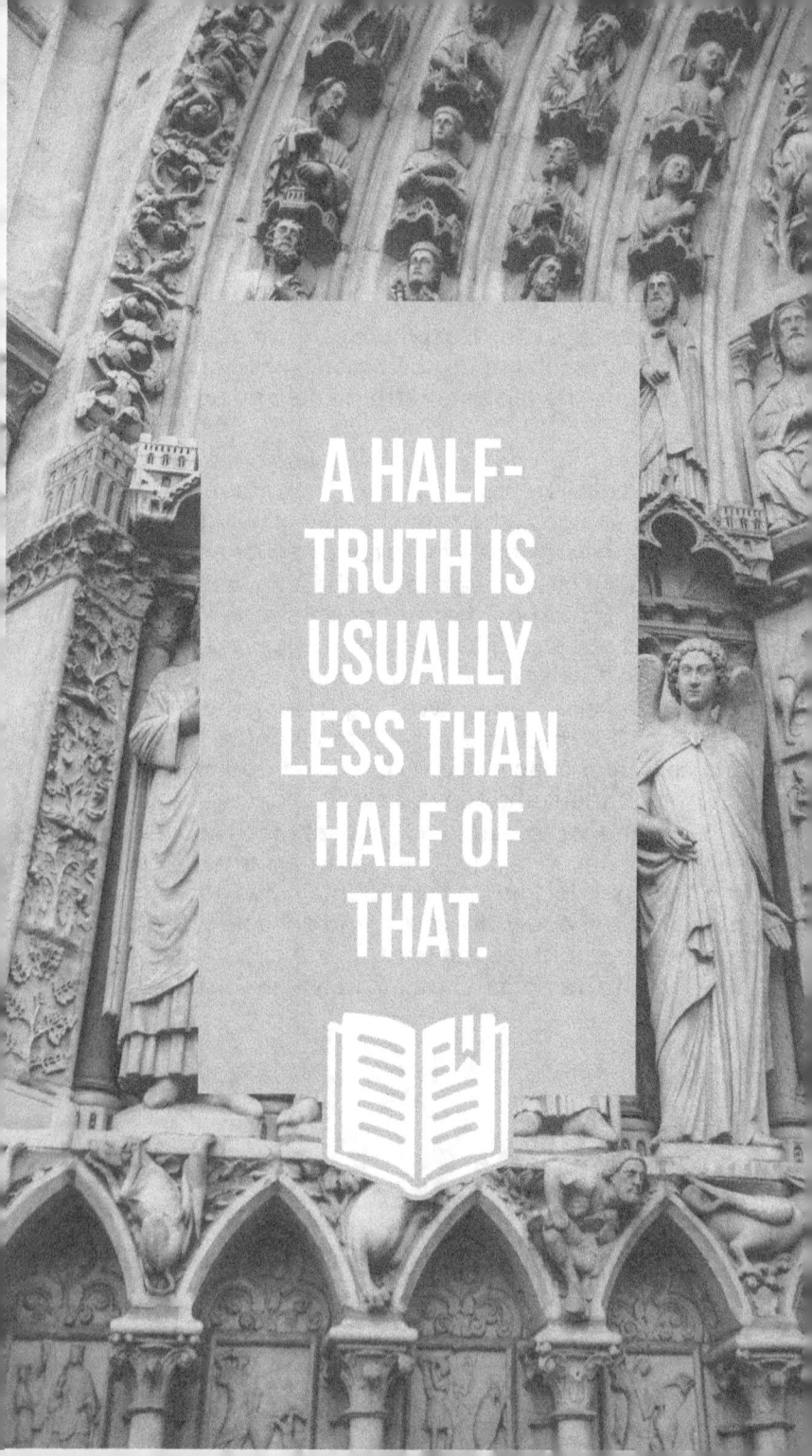

A HALF-TRUTH IS USUALLY LESS THAN HALF OF THAT.

A missionary in Brazil once ran a camp near the Parana River. On days when the temperature reached a scorching 120 degrees, he was tempted to swim in the cool river waters, but was leery because of the man-eating fish that he knew inhabited the river. His neighbors assured him, however, that piranhas only bite people while swimming in schools and that they never swam in schools in that part of the river. So each afternoon for the rest of the summer, the missionary enjoyed a swim.

Months later, the missionary heard a report that a local fisherman had fallen out of his boat and had not been found. Alarmed, he asked his neighbors if perhaps the man had been eaten by piranhas. "Oh, no," they said. "Only while swimming in schools do piranhas bite people, and they never swim in schools around here."

"But why not around here?" the missionary pressed.

"Oh," his neighbor casually replied, "they never swim in schools in places where there are alligators."[38]

It's always important when hearing things you want to hear—especially statements that offer reassurance, flattery, or approval—that you question what is not being said. The whole truth always acknowledges the negative.

The Lord detests lying lips, but he delights in men who are truthful.

PROVERBS 12:22 NIV

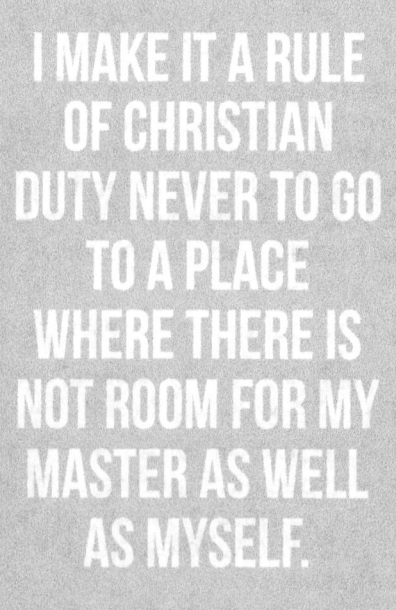

I MAKE IT A RULE
OF CHRISTIAN
DUTY NEVER TO GO
TO A PLACE
WHERE THERE IS
NOT ROOM FOR MY
MASTER AS WELL
AS MYSELF.

A young farmer in the West had a reputation for frequenting the local bar, which was located in the town's hotel. Then, he was converted to Christ. Whenever he visited town, however, he continued to tie his team of horses to the hotel hitching post. An elderly deacon from the town church couldn't help but notice this practice. He said, "George, I'm a good deal older than you, and I know you will pardon me if I make a suggestion from my experience. No matter how strong you think you are, take my advice and change your hitching post at once."[39]

There are times when "changing your hitching post" is an important part of one's Christian witness. A couple in a sophisticated urban area discovered this in a slightly different way after their conversion. They had long been part of a social set in which alcohol freely flowed. After their conversion, they discovered that when they tried to tell their friends about Christ, they were highly ineffective as long as they were holding glasses in their hands—even though their glasses contained a soft drink. When they switched to holding coffee cups, however, people noticed the changes in the rest of their behavior, which gave credibility to their testimony.

When you proclaim Christ in your life, people expect to see a difference in how you act.

Don't be teamed with those who do not love the Lord . . . How can a Christian be a partner with one who doesn't believe?

2 CORINTHIANS 6:14, 15 TLB

JESUS CAN TURN WATER INTO WINE, BUT HE CAN'T TURN YOUR WHINING INTO ANYTHING.

Astronaut Shannon Lucid was not supposed to set an American record for time spent in space. However, her assignment was extended one and a half months because of technical difficulties with shuttle booster rockets and two hurricanes. The result was that Lucid stayed in space 188 days, setting a U.S. space endurance record and a world record for a woman. She returned to earth to high accolades from politicians and NASA officials, as well as to the loving arms of her family members.

What many reports failed to note in the wake of Lucid's record-setting stay on the Russian space station Mir, was the excellent reputation that Lucid had with her Russian hosts. That reputation was based not only on her technical expertise as an astronaut, but on the fact that her Russian counterparts never once heard her complain during her six-month stay. Every time Lucid was notified of a shuttle delay, she took the news in stride.

Valery Ryumin, a Russian space manager, noted that Lucid reacted like Russian cosmonauts do when their missions are extended: Russians deliberately choose cosmonauts "who are strong enough not to show any feelings" when receiving bad news.[40]

Complaining not only makes you feel negative, but it spreads your negativity to others. Even an unpleasant or disappointing situation can become positive when you have a good attitude and speak uplifting words.

Do all things without murmurings and disputings.

PHILIPPIANS 2:14

OBSTACLES
ARE THOSE
FRIGHTFUL
THINGS YOU SEE
WHEN YOU TAKE
YOUR EYES OFF
THE GOAL.

Kenneth was a high school football star and later, an avid wrestler, boxer, hunter, and skin-diver. Then, a broken neck sustained in a wrestling match left him paralyzed from the chest down. He underwent therapy and his doctors were hopeful that one day he would be able to walk with the help of braces and crutches.

The former athlete could not reconcile himself to his physical limitations, however, so he prevailed upon two of his best friends to take him in his wheelchair to a wooded area. They left him alone there with a twelve-gauge shotgun. After they left, he held the shotgun to his abdomen and pulled the trigger. He committed suicide at the age of twenty-four.

At the age of nineteen, Jim was stabbed, leaving him paralyzed from the middle of his chest down. Although confined to a wheelchair, he lives alone, cooks his own meals, washes his clothes, and cleans his house. He drives himself in his specially equipped automobile. He has written three books, and was the photographer for the first book on the history of wheelchair sports. Thirty years after his injury, he made a successful parachute jump, landing precisely on his target.[41]

Kevin and Jim had nearly identical injuries and physical limitations. Their outlook, however, led to vastly different outcomes. What is your outlook on life today?

And he (Jesus) said, "Come." And when Peter was come down out of the ship, he walked on the water, to go to Jesus. But when he saw the wind boisterous, he was afraid; and beginning to sink, he cried, saying, "Lord, save me." And immediately Jesus stretched forth his hand, and caught him.

MATTHEW 14:29-31

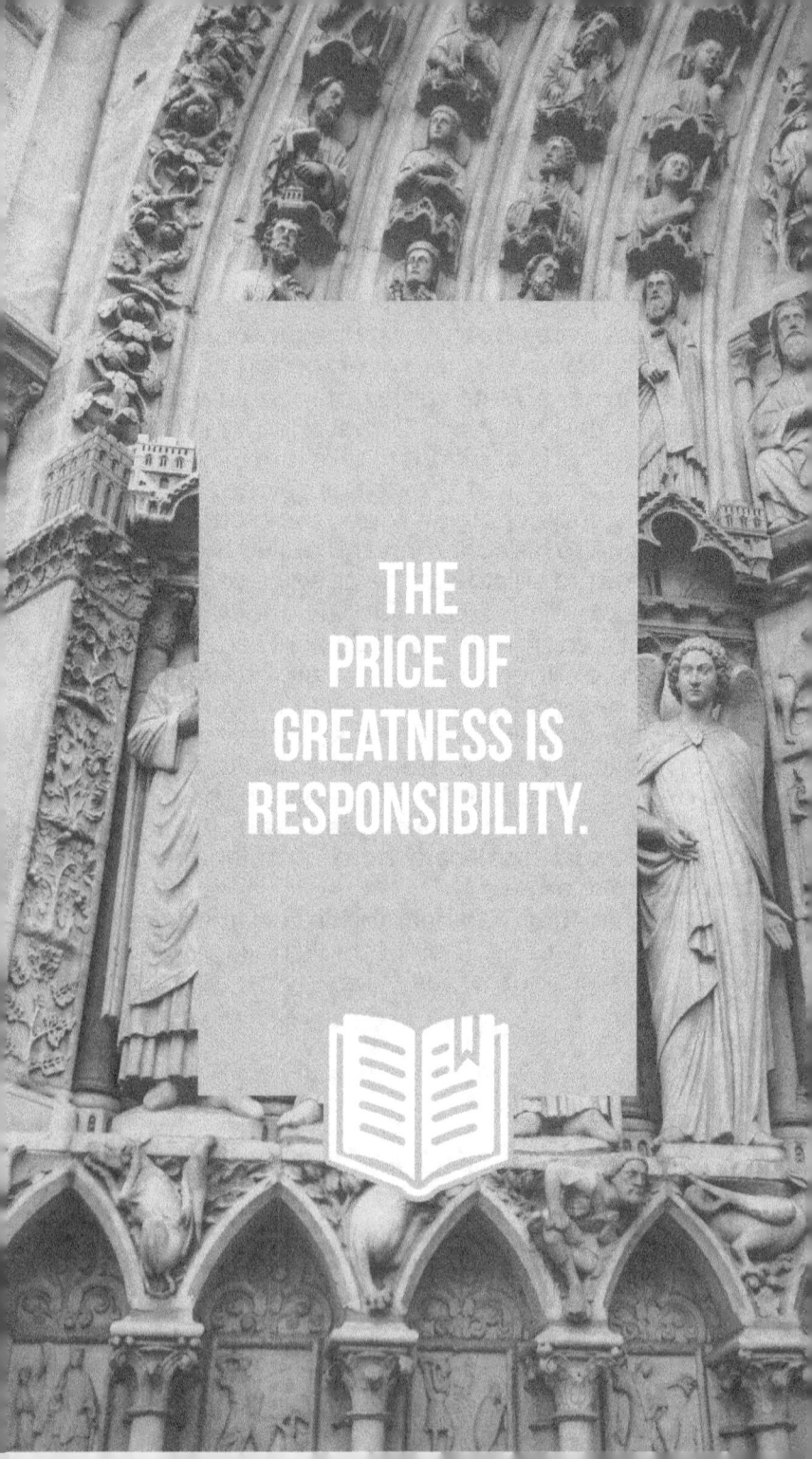

THE
PRICE OF
GREATNESS IS
RESPONSIBILITY.

C harles Lamb was once deeply in love with a woman, but he never married. Rather, he willingly chose to fill the role of "guardian angel" of his childhood home, and especially of his sister Mary, who at times was mentally deranged. He saw his foremost responsibilities in life as those of son and brother.

After Mary stabbed their mother to death in one of her mad spells, Charles turned away from any pursuits that might have furthered or enhanced his own life, and for thirty-eight years he watched over Mary with tender care. A friend has told how he sometimes would see the brother and sister walking hand in hand across the field to the old asylum, their faces bathed in tears.

The story of Charles Lamb is a sad story, yet a grand one. He had a purpose in life, he had a role —and it was never left empty.[42]

In our self-centered world, we tend to dismiss the greatness of people like Charles Lamb. And yet without those who make such sacrifices, there is little we could count as noble or admirable in our culture. It is the willingness to take on responsibilities that require selfless giving that truly makes a person great.

"But he that is greatest among you shall be your servant."

MATTHEW 23:11

DEVOTING A LITTLE
OF YOURSELF TO
EVERYTHING
MEANS
COMMITTING A
GREAT DEAL OF
YOURSELF TO
NOTHING.

Linda was a perfectionist as a wife and mother, kept a spotless house, served excellent meals, and was a willing volunteer at church, her children's school, and in the community. She tried to be all things to all people, and was often frustrated and physically exhausted. Still, she was unwilling to give up any of her commitments or lower her standards. She felt she needed to be perfect and do everything she did in order to keep her husband's love.

A crisis came for Linda when her husband told her he would leave her if she *didn't* slow down and give up some of her responsibilities. She responded in anger and assumed even more responsibility than before. She was eventually hospitalized for exhaustion.

While in the hospital, Linda feared things would go to pieces in her absence from her home and community. When she saw that the world did indeed go on without her—her children still wore clean clothes, meals were still cooked, the various boards and committees continued to function—Linda began to relax for the first time in years. The result was not only the restoration of her own health, but her relationship with her family was strengthened.[43]

Choose to do what you do well, but make your choices wisely, and limit them to what is truly required.

Whatsoever thy hand findeth to do, do it with thy might.

ECCLESIASTES 9:10

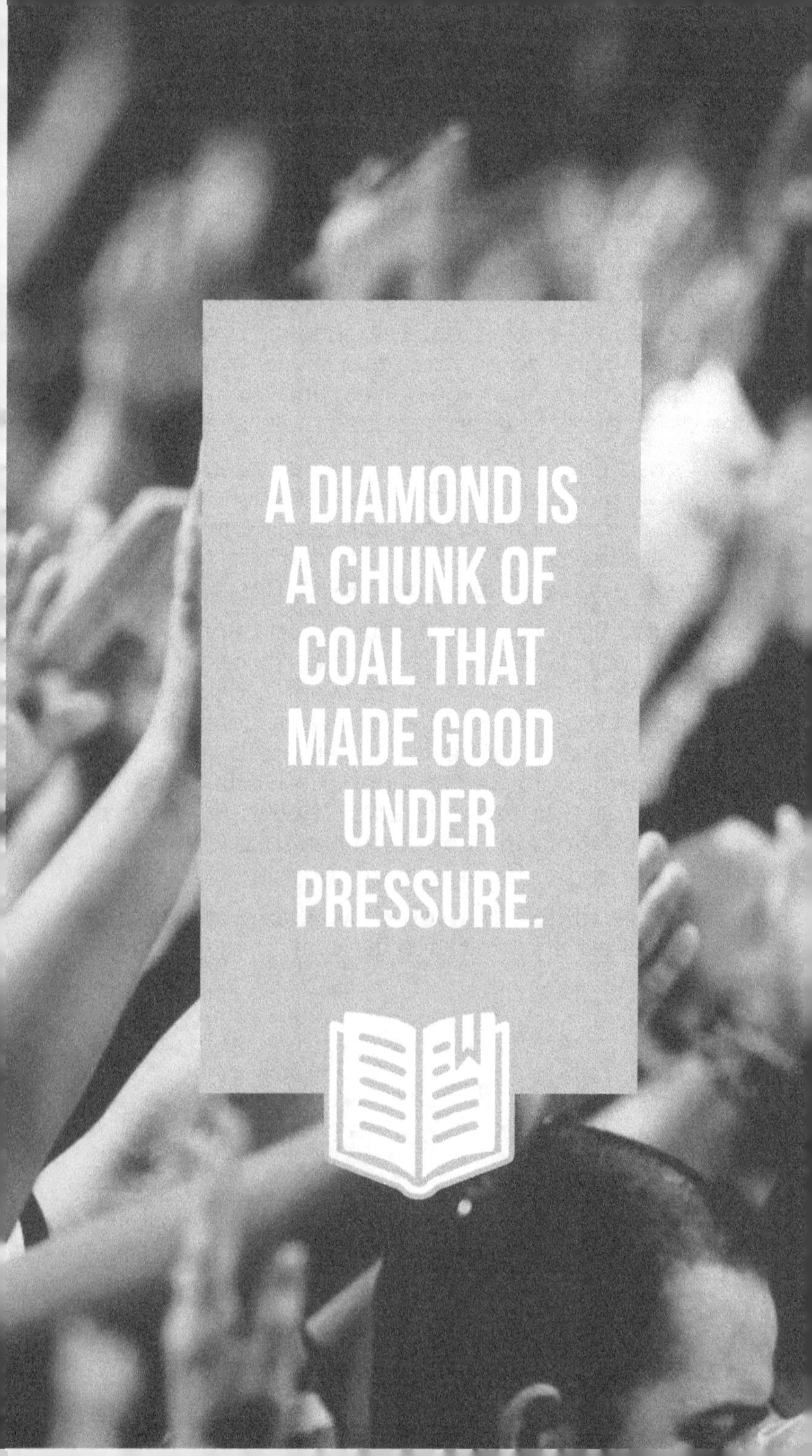

A DIAMOND IS
A CHUNK OF
COAL THAT
MADE GOOD
UNDER
PRESSURE.

Bernie Marcus was a poor Russian cabinet-maker's son from Newark, New Jersey. Arthur Blank was raised in a lower-middle-class neighborhood in Queens, New York. Blank once ran with a juvenile gang and his father died when he was only fifteen. He has said, "I grew up with the notion that life is going to be filled with some storms."

In 1978, Marcus and Blank worked together at a hardware store in Los Angeles. The store was taken over by a new owner, who fired them both. The day after they lost their jobs, an investor friend suggested they go into business for themselves.

Marcus recalls, "Once I stopped stewing in my misery, I saw that the idea wasn't so crazy." Marcus and Blank opened the kind of store they had always dreaded competing against: a no-frills, hangar-size outlet with a huge selection and high-grade service. Today, their Home Depot stores are at the top of the fast-growing home-improvement industry.

Marcus enjoys talking to other entrepreneurs. He often asks them, "Was there a point in your life when you despaired?" He once was quoted as saying, "I've discussed this with fifty successful entrepreneurs. Forty had that character-building experience."[44]

Consider your "low time" to be a position from which to rebound, not the place where you plan to stay!

Consider it all joy . . . when you encounter various trials; knowing that the testing of your faith produces endurance. And let endurance have its perfect result, that you may be perfect and complete, lacking in nothing.

JAMES 1:2-4 NASB

THE SMALLEST DEED IS BETTER THAN THE GREATEST INTENTION!

Giving is like a two-sided coin. The more we "open up" in our attitude toward giving, the more our attitude toward seeing the blessings that God has and is pouring into our lives "opens up." But, the secret to activating this principle appears to be giving without desiring public acclaim. Our giving must be "pride free." This principle is captured well in a poem by an unknown author:

I did a favor yesterday,
A kindly little deed,
And then I called to all the world
To stop and look and heed.

They stopped and looked and flattered me
In words I could not trust,
And when the world had gone away
My good deed turned to dust.

A very tiny courtesy I found to do today;
Twas quickly done with none to see
And then I ran away

But someone must have witnessed it,
For—truly—I declare
As I sped back the stony path
Roses were blooming there.[45]

Let us not love [merely] in theory or in speech but in deed and in truth—in practice and in sincerity.

1 JOHN 3:18 AMP

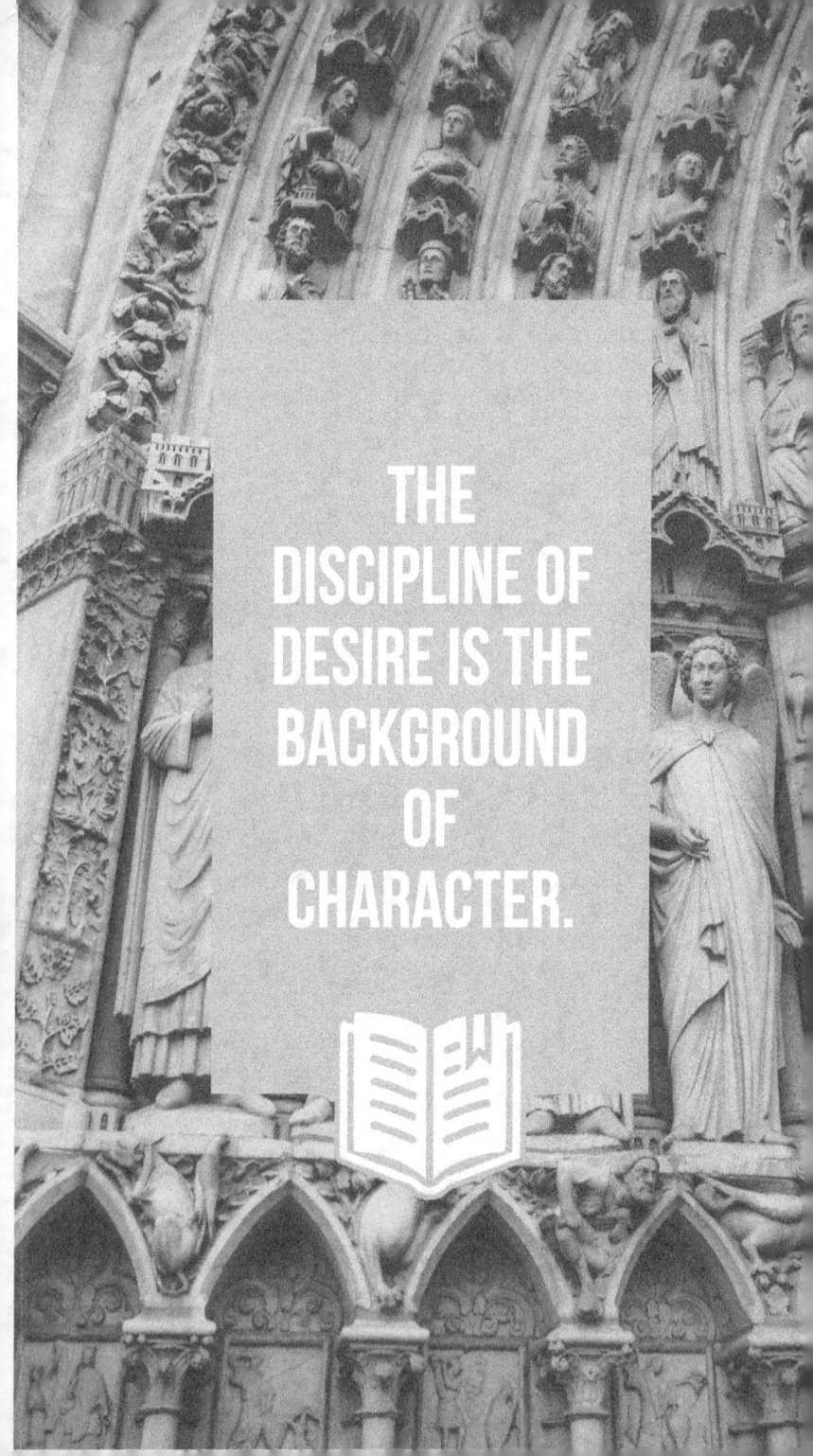

THE
DISCIPLINE OF
DESIRE IS THE
BACKGROUND
OF
CHARACTER.

In *Sin, Sex and Self-Control,* Norman Vincent Peale writes: "Martha took the kids away to the mountains for a month, so I was a summer bachelor. And about midway through that month I met a girl, a beautiful girl looking for excitement. She made it clear that I had a green light . . . so for one weekend I put my conscience in mothballs and arranged a meeting with her for Saturday night.

"I woke up early Saturday morning with a bit of a hangover; I'd played poker until late the night before. I decided to get up, put on my swimming trunks, and take a walk on the beach to clear my head. I took an ax along, because the wreck of an old barge had come ashore down the beach, and there was a lot of tangled rope that was worth salvaging . . . There was something about the freshness of the morning and the feel of the ax that made me want to keep on swinging it. So I began to chop in earnest."

As he chopped, a strange thing began to happen. He said, "I felt as if I were outside myself, looking at myself through a kind of fog that was gradually clearing. And suddenly I knew that what I had been planning for that evening was so wrong, so out of key with my standards and my loyalties and the innermost me that it was out of the question." He canceled the date.[46]

Step back and take a good look at yourself. Is there something you need to get a clear view on today?

> But I keep under my body, and bring it into subjection: lest that by any means, when I have preached to others, I myself should be a castaway.
>
> 1 CORINTHIANS 9:27

YOU CAN BUILD
A THRONE WITH
BAYONETS,
BUT YOU CAN'T
SIT ON IT FOR
LONG.

Ben was disgusted with himself for having let the bill grow so large. He was a home-delivery milkman and had allowed a pretty young woman with six children and another on the way to fall $79 behind on her account. She told him repeatedly, "I'm going to pay you soon, when my husband gets a second job." Ben believed her. But eventually she moved away and left no forwarding address. He was angry that he had been so gullible, and even more angry about the loss of the $79, which would have to come from his own pocket.

A friend made an unusual suggestion: "Give the milk to the woman. Make it a Christmas present to the kids who needed it."

Ben replied, "Are you kidding? I don't even get my wife a Christmas gift that expensive."

"Perhaps not," the friend said, "but you've already lost the income. What do you have to lose?"

Ben resisted the idea, but in the end, he told his friend, "I did it! I gave her the milk as a Christmas present. It wasn't easy, but I really do feel better. Those kids had lots of milk on their cereal just because of me." He not only felt better toward the woman, but toward all his customers. His cheerful nature was restored.[47]

The best way to deal with those who "do you wrong," is to "do them right."

So are the ways of everyone who gains by violence; it takes away the life of its possessors.

PROVERBS 1:19 NASB

YOU CAN'T FILL AN EMPTY BUCKET WITH A DRY WELL.

There are three kinds of givers: the flint, the sponge, and the honeycomb.

To get anything from the flint, you must hammer it. And even then, you generally get only chips and sparks. It gives nothing away if it can help it, and even then only with a great display.

To get anything from the sponge, you must squeeze it. It is good-natured. It readily yields to pressure, and the more it is pressed, the more it gives. Still, one must press.

To get anything from the honeycomb, one must only take what flows from it. It takes delight in giving, without pressure, without begging or badgering. It gives its sweetness freely.

There is another difference in the honeycomb. It is a renewable resource. Unlike the flint or sponge, the honeycomb is connected to life—it is the product of ongoing work and creative energy.

One of the reasons "honeycomb givers" are able to give freely, is that they are aware that their lives are continually being replenished. They believe that what they give away will soon be regenerated.[48]

As long as you are connected to the Source of all giving, you can never run dry. When you give freely you will receive in like manner.

"He who believes in Me, as the Scripture said, 'From his innermost being shall flow rivers of living water.'"

JOHN 7:38 NASB

I'VE SUFFERED
A GREAT MANY
CATASTROPHES
IN MY LIFE.
MOST OF THEM
NEVER
HAPPENED.

A man was driving down a country road late one night, when his tire blew out. He opened his trunk only to discover he had forgotten to replace the jack the last time he had used it. He saw the light from a farmhouse in the distance and began walking toward it, hoping to borrow a jack. On the way, he mused, *I'll knock on the door and say I'm in trouble and would you please lend me a jack. He'll say sure.*

As he walked, however, he noticed that the light in the house had gone out. He thought to himself, *Now he's gone to bed and he'll be mad because I've awakened him. I'd better offer him a dollar for his trouble.*

The man continued the imaginary conversation in his head as he walked. *What if he is away and his wife is alone? She'll be afraid to open the door. I'd better offer five dollars.* This amount, however, seemed too high. *Five dollars! All right, but not a cent more. What are you trying to do, rob a man?* By this time he was on the porch of the farmhouse.

He knocked loudly. When the farmer in residence leaned out the upstairs window and asked, "Who's there?" the stranger yelled back at him, "You and your stupid jack! You can keep the wretched thing!"[49]

Much of the struggle in life comes not from actual circumstances we encounter, but from our overactive imaginations.

For God hath not given us the spirit of fear; but of power, and of love, and of a sound mind.

2 TIMOTHY 1:7

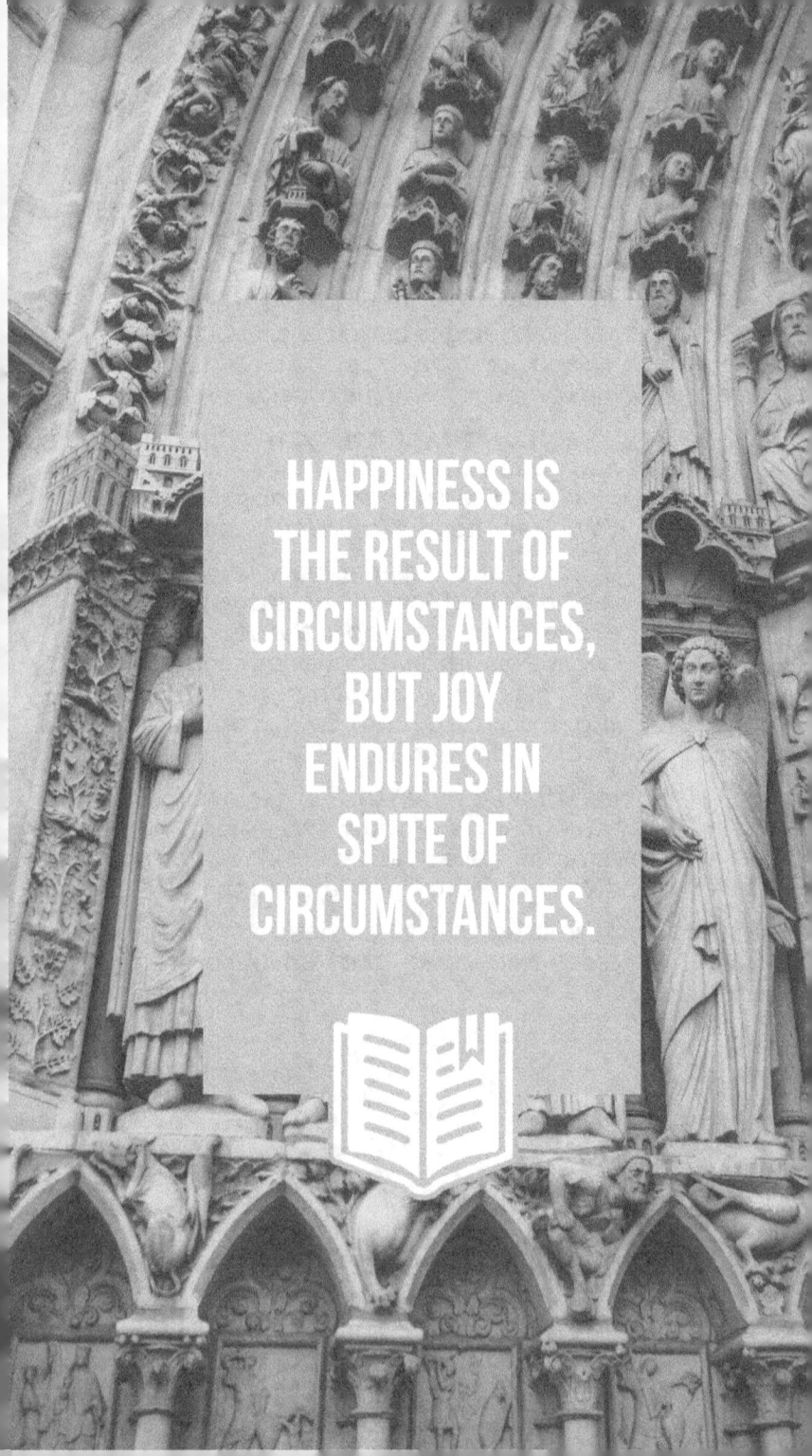

HAPPINESS IS
THE RESULT OF
CIRCUMSTANCES,
BUT JOY
ENDURES IN
SPITE OF
CIRCUMSTANCES.

One Christmas Eve, a man was driving two young women to a church youth group celebration when they came upon a multiple-car collision. They were unable to stop on the slick road before they slammed into the back of a car. One of the girls, Donna, was thrown face-first through the windshield. The jagged edges of the broken windshield made two deep gashes in her left cheek.

At the hospital, the doctor on duty happened to be a plastic surgeon. He took great care in stitching Donna's face. Nevertheless, the driver was devastated by what had happened and dreaded visiting Donna on Christmas Day. He expected to find her sad and depressed. Instead, he found her happy and bright, asking many questions of her doctors and nurses. A nurse confided to him that all the nurses were making excuses to go into Donna's room—they called her a "ray of sunshine." She refused to let the accident destroy her Christmas joy.

The man moved to another city shortly thereafter and lost touch with the family—for fifteen years. When he saw Donna's mother again, he fearfully asked how Donna was doing. Her mother told him that Donna had been so intrigued by her hospital stay that she became a nurse, got a good job at a hospital, met a young doctor, married him, and then had two children.

The mother said, "Donna told me to tell you that the accident was the best thing that could have happened to her!"[50]

We have the freedom to choose our attitude in any and every circumstance of life. We can choose to let trouble leave us depressed and weak, or we can choose to be happy and strong in spite of our trials. When we choose to have joy, our worst moments can be turned into our greatest triumphs.

In thy presence is fullness of joy; at thy right hand there are pleasures for evermore.

PSALM 16:11

ONE REASON
THE DOG HAS SO
MANY FRIENDS:
HE WAGS HIS
TAIL INSTEAD
OF HIS TONGUE.

G ossip usually begins because a person feels a need for attention or revenge. A better way to get attention, however, is to speak and do good. The "best" revenge is found in doing good to one's enemies.

If you were busy being kind,
Before you knew it, you would find
You had forgotten to think 'twas true
That someone was unkind to you.

If you were busy, being glad
And cheering people who were sad,
You'd soon forget to notice it,
Although your heart might ache a bit.

If you were busy being good,
And doing just the best you could,
You won't have the time to blame
Someone doing just the best he can.

If you were busy being true
To what you know you ought to do,
You'd be so busy you'd forget
The blunders of the folks you've met.[51]

Choose today to stay busy showing kindness, spreading cheer, and doing your best. You not only will have no time or temptation to gossip, but others will find little to gossip about in your life!

An evil man sows strife; gossip separates the best of friends.

PROVERBS 16:28 TLB

WHAT A BIG DIFFERENCE THERE IS BETWEEN GIVING ADVICE AND LENDING A HAND.

The story is told of a young man who chose to take on a problem that plagues many American cities: potholes. In his case, the problem was one particular pothole. It was located at an intersection near his home, and it had been there for as long as he could remember. Residents of the neighborhood had developed the habit of driving around it; strangers learned about it the hard way.

One day, the young man decided it was time to fix the problem. He and his brother stopped in at a hardware store and purchased sand and cement. Once the store owner learned what they planned to do, he loaned them a shovel and a concrete mixer, and even volunteered his son to help out.

As soon as they began filling in the pothole, several passing motorists parked their cars and began directing traffic around the three men at work. Some passing children made "Wet Concrete" signs to put around the pothole once the work was done. In all, nearly twenty neighbors participated in the project. Together, they had handled a problem that had bothered all of them for years. All it took was one person willing to step forward and take responsibility for seeing that the problem was fixed.[52]

It's one thing to define a problem or theorize about solutions, it's quite another to actually solve the problem!

Little children, let us stop just saying we love people, let us really love them, and show it by our actions.

1 JOHN 3:18 TLB

THE MAN WHO
PAYS AN OUNCE
OF PRINCIPLE
FOR A POUND OF
POPULARITY
GETS BADLY
CHEATED.

In ancient Greece, one of the most politically crafty philosophers was Aristippus. He also had a hearty appetite for the "good life." Although Aristippus disagreed with the tyrant, Denys, who ruled over the region, he had learned how to get along with him in court by flattering him on all occasions. Aristippus looked down his nose at some of the less prosperous philosophers and wise men who refused to stoop that low.

One day, Aristippus saw his colleague Diogenes washing some vegetables. He said to him disdainfully, "If you would only learn to flatter King Denys you would not have to be washing lentils."

Diogenes looked up slowly and in the same tone of voice replied, "And you, if you had only learned to live on lentils, would not have to flatter King Denys."[53]

Flattery is a two-edged sword: lying and manipulation. A genuine compliment is always in order, but flattery is telling a person something that isn't true in hopes of gaining their favor. What the flatterer doesn't realize, of course, is that with each falsehood, he is diminishing his own value. Eventually his words have no meaning and his flattery sounds hollow, even to the one who has been flattered.

Choose instead to be a person of principle—one who always speaks the truth, with love.

"For they loved the praise of men more than the praise of God."

JOHN 12:43

THE HEART
HAS NO
SECRET WHICH
OUR CONDUCT
DOES NOT
REVEAL.

The oldest sister of Daniel Webster was married to John Colby, who was considered the most wicked, godless man in his neighborhood when it came to swearing and impiety. Then news came to Webster that there was a change in Colby. He decided to call on him to see if it was true.

On entering his sister's home, he noticed a large-print Bible opened on a table. Colby had been reading it before he answered Webster's knock on the door. The first question Colby asked him was, "Are you a Christian?" When he was assured of Webster's faith, he suggested that they kneel together and pray.

After the visit, Webster told a friend, "I would like to hear what enemies of religion say of Colby's conversion. Here was a man as unlikely to be a Christian as any I ever saw; and he had gone his godless way until now, with old age and habits hard to change! Yet see him—a penitent, trusting, humble believer! Nothing short of the grace of Almighty God."[54]

The fruit of your faith is always found in your behavior. You cannot hide what you believe, or don't believe. Your actions will always give away the secrets of your heart.

"The good man brings good things out of the good stored up in him, and the evil man brings evil things out of the evil stored up in him."

MATTHEW 12:36 NIV

GUILT IS
CONCERNED WITH
THE PAST.
WORRY IS
CONCERNED ABOUT
THE FUTURE.
CONTENTMENT
ENJOYS THE
PRESENT.

n *A Man Called Peter*, Catherine Marshall writes about the angst her son felt in moving from kindergarten to the first grade. "Peter John was stunned to discover that something new had been added. The first grade was no longer all play. He was expected to learn to read and write. He questioned us sharply about this none-too-welcome change. 'You might as well get used to it, Peter,' his father said bluntly; 'you'll have to go to school for a long time—eleven years, then four more years of college, then maybe more.'

"Peter looked crushed, and went away disconsolate. It took him several weeks to get used to this new and awful revelation. He would be sitting on the floor playing with his wooden trains and blocks, apparently quite content, when suddenly his lower lip would begin to tremble, and tears would overflow. 'Peter, what on earth is the matter?' we would question. Between sobs he would say, 'I'm worryin' about when I'll have to go to college . . .'"

Marshall felt her son's behavior could reveal something about worry to all of us. She wrote, "The next time you start fretting about something, rather than trusting God to take care of it, remember that an all-wise God knows your worrying to be just as futile—just as silly—as our six-year-old worrying about when he will go to college."[55]

Not that I am implying that I was in any personal want; for I have learned how to be content (satisfied to the point where I am not disturbed or disquieted) in whatever state I am.

PHILIPPIANS 4:11 AMP

SOME PEOPLE ARE ALWAYS GRUMBLING BECAUSE ROSES HAVE THORNS; I AM THANKFUL THAT THORNS HAVE ROSES.

Robert and his wife were in shock when their dream cabin—10,000 square feet of luxurious space overlooking Mount Timpanogos —was crushed in an avalanche. It took nature only ten seconds to destroy what had taken them several years to design, plan, build, and furnish. They had a very difficult time seeing God in the situation as they picked through the smashed bits of their belongings.

Eight months later, Robert was at a business meeting when a colleague told him about an accident their wives had almost had on the day of the avalanche. Before leaving their cabin, one of this man's sons had offered a prayer for a safe trip home. Then, as they drove down the narrow road, they met Robert's wife but when they slammed on their brakes, the car skidded on the ice. Just before the two vehicles collided, the man's wife turned her Suburban into a deep snow bank. It took almost an hour to get the vehicle unstuck—all that time it blocked Robert's wife and son from passing. Had the accident not occurred, Robert's wife and child would very likely have been at home, killed in the avalanche![56]

Be slow to judge devastating circumstances in your life. Trouble does not come from God, but He is ever-present to turn those things around for your good. Ask God to show you His hand in the situation and you will see that He was there helping you all along.

Offer to God the sacrifice of thanksgiving.

PSALM 50:14 AMP

THE NEXT TIME YOU FEEL LIKE COMPLAINING, REMEMBER THAT YOUR GARBAGE DISPOSAL PROBABLY EATS BETTER THAN 30 PERCENT OF THE PEOPLE IN THIS WORLD.

The World Health Organization has estimated that approximately one-third of the world is well-fed, one-third is underfed, and one-third is starving. Worldwide, four million people die of starvation each year and 70 percent of children under age six are undernourished. At this rate, thirty people die of starvation every minute.

The United Nations Food and Agricultural Organization has reported: "About 460 million people are at the brink of starvation daily and some 200 million children slip into some form of mental retardation and blindness due to lack of food, another ten million or so give way finally to hunger-related diseases."

In 1975, U.S. Senator Mark O. Hatfield presented a resolution designating the Monday before Thanksgiving Day as a "National Day of Fasting." He and Stan Mooneyham, then President of World Vision International, called on all Americans to willingly experience hunger and reevaluate their own lifestyles and habits.[57]

When you are tempted to complain about something you don't have, stop and remind yourself to be thankful for what you do have. God will reward your thankfulness.

Let your conversation be without covetousness; and be content with such things as ye have.

HEBREWS 13:5

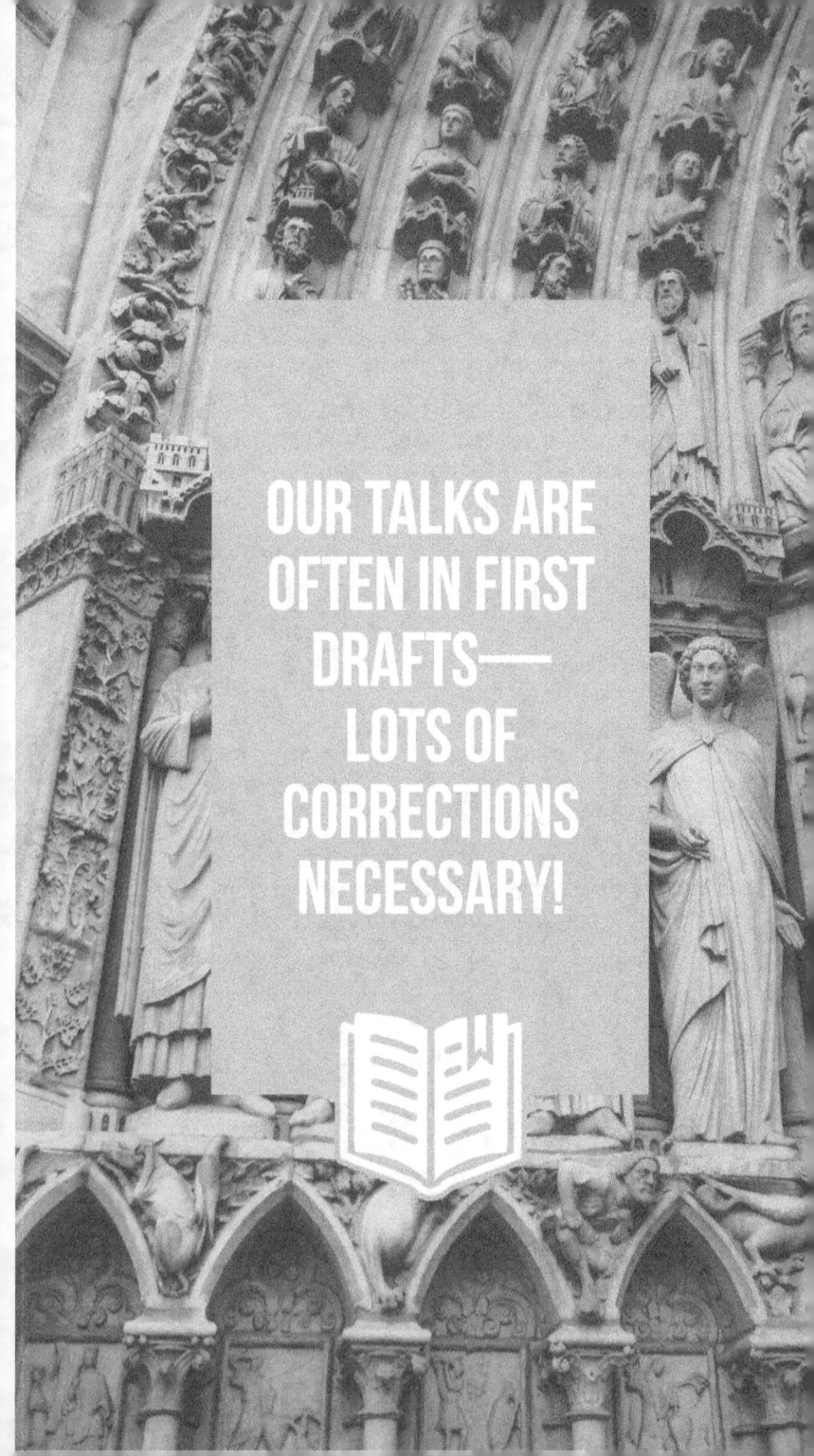

OUR TALKS ARE OFTEN IN FIRST DRAFTS—LOTS OF CORRECTIONS NECESSARY!

I t's not easy to control our tongues. But as these words from the poem, "Drop a Pebble in the Water," by James W. Foley illustrate, a careless word can have far-reaching effects. Fortunately, so can a careful word!

> Drop a pebble in the water: just a splash, and it is gone;
> But there's half-a-hundred ripples circling on and on and on,
> Spreading, spreading from the center, flowing on out to the sea.
> And there is no way of telling where the end is going to be.
> Drop an unkind word, or careless: in a minute it is gone;
> But there's half-a-hundred ripples circling on and on and on.
> They keep spreading, spreading, spreading from the center as they go,
> And there is no way to stop them, once you've started them to flow.
> Drop a word of cheer and kindness: in a minute you forget;
> But there's gladness still a-swelling, and there's joy a-circling yet,
> And you've rolled a wave of comfort whose sweet music can be heard
> Over miles and miles of water just by dropping one kind word.[58]

For in many things we offend all. If any man offend not in word, the same is a perfect man, and able also to bridle the whole body.

JAMES 3:2

MOST OF THE
SHADOWS OF
THIS LIFE ARE
CAUSED BY
STANDING IN
ONE'S OWN
SUNSHINE.

Antonio Salieri, an ambitious, albeit mediocre 18th-century composer offers this prayer in the popular film on Mozart's life, *Amadeus*:

Lord, make me a great composer. Let me celebrate Your glory through music. And be celebrated myself. Make me famous through the world, dear God, make me immortal. After I die, let people speak my name forever with love for what I wrote. In return I will give You my chastity, my industry, my deep humility, my life.

When it became obvious to the superficially pious Salieri that he would never be as gifted as the roguish Wolfgang Amadeus Mozart, he became insanely jealous of Mozart and plotted to destroy him. He also turned from God. As far as Salieri was concerned, God had betrayed him. He had failed to answer his prayer. In a very powerful scene in the movie, he takes a cru-cifix from the wall of his room and places it in the fire.[59]

Even when a person seems to be successful in doing great things for God, he may find that he feels unfulfilled. When that happens, pride is generally at work. The person desires God to use him in a special way, for his own glory, without realizing that true fulfillment lies in allowing God to use us in any way He desires, for His glory.

A man's pride shall bring him low; but honour shall uphold the humble in spirit.

PROVERBS 29:23

DEATH IS NOT A PERIOD BUT A COMMA IN THE STORY OF LIFE.

One of the most ancient books in the Bible is the Book of Job. In it, Job poses a question that has been in man's heart from the beginning: "If a man die, shall he live again?"

Many answers have been offered through the centuries:

Science says, "A person may live again."

Philosophy says, "Every person hopes to live again."

Ethics says, "He ought to live again."

Atheism says, "He will never live again."

Reincarnationists say, "He will live again but in another form, not as himself."

Judaism says, "He will live on in his children and in the memory of all he has befriended."

Jesus Christ said, "He shall live again if he believes in Me. I am the resurrection and the life."[60]

Regardless of your denominational or religious persuasion, death is something you will face—either with or without the hope of eternal life.

The truly amazing thing for those who believe in Christ Jesus is that the hope of eternal life offered by Him is what gives hope to their *daily* life. When eternal life is your hope, you can face every day with joy.

Jesus said unto her (Martha), "I am the resurrection, and the life: he that believeth in me, though he were dead, yet shall he live: And whosoever liveth and believeth in me shall never die."

JOHN 11:25,26

TO KNOW THE WILL OF
GOD IS THE GREATEST
KNOWLEDGE,
TO FIND THE WILL OF
GOD IS THE GREATEST
DISCOVERY,
AND TO DO THE WILL
OF GOD IS THE
GREATEST
ACHIEVEMENT.

It was late and she was tired. She had been working all day and she needed to leave town early the following morning. She was scheduled to give three talks in two cities in one day. But Eugenia Price was prevailed upon to talk with someone—an actor who couldn't overcome his addiction to alcohol.

Before she agreed to meet with the man, Eugenia struggled with doubts. *Was it fair to the people she'd he speaking to the next day to exhaust herself now and not give her best? The actor lived near her home—perhaps she could talk with him after she returned from her trip.*

Finally, she asked God to reveal to her His will for the man for that night. After praying quietly for several minutes, she knew what to do. She spoke with the actor, believing God had asked her to do so.

On his way home from their meeting that night, the actor stopped his car on the side of the road and asked Jesus to be his Savior and Lord. What had brought him to that point? He said he was impressed by the fact that despite her weariness and doubts, Eugenia had been mastered by Jesus. She had put her will into His hands and trusted Him to lead her in the right direction.[61]

For one actor, one woman's decision to do God's will on one night made an eternal difference.

"If any one would serve Me, he must continue to follow Me—to cleave steadfastly to Me, conform wholly to My example, in living . . . and wherever I am, there will My servant be also. If anyone serves Me, the Father will honor him."

JOHN 12:26 AMP

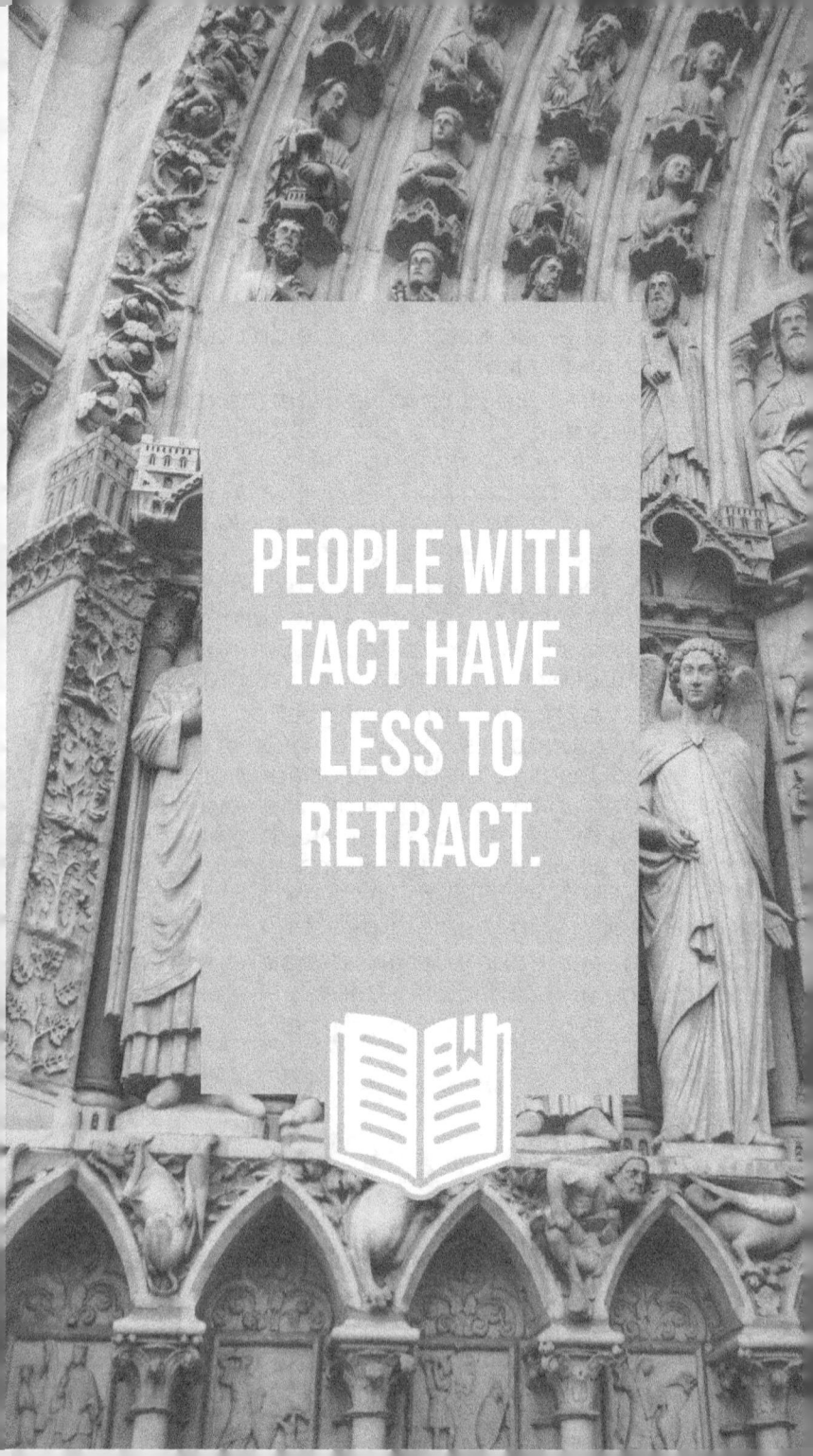

PEOPLE WITH TACT HAVE LESS TO RETRACT.

A young preacher had announced to his congregation that he was leaving the church to accept another call. He was standing at the door after the service to greet the people, as preachers often do, when one of the elderly saints approached him. Her eyes were swimming with tears as she said, "Oh, pastor, I'm so sorry you've decided to leave. Things will never be the same again." The young man was flattered. Taking her hands in his, he replied with as much kindness as possible, "Bless you, dear sister, but I'm sure that God will send you a new pastor even better than I." She choked back a sob as she said, "That's what they all say, but they keep getting worse and worse."

Another woman was overheard telling her pastor after a worship service, "I'm deaf, and I hardly hear a word you preach, but I still come to get my plate full." Hoping to console her, this pastor said, "Well, maybe you haven't missed much." She replied, "Yes, that's what they all tell me."[62]

The old adage "think before you speak" is still the best way to fulfill the equally long-standing advice, "If you can't say something good, don't say anything at all."

The heart of the righteous weighs its answers, but the mouth of the wicked gushes evil.

PROVERBS 15:28 NIV

IF THE GRASS
LOOKS GREENER
ON THE OTHER
SIDE OF THE
FENCE, YOU CAN
BET THE WATER
BILL IS HIGHER.

Several years ago, columnist Jim Bishop reported what had happened to several families who had won their state's lottery.

Rosa won $400 a week for life in the Washington lottery. She hides in her apartment. For the first time in her life, she struggles with nerves. Everyone tries to get something from her. She has said, "People are so mean. I hope you win the lottery and see what happens to you."

The McGugarts were ecstatic when Pop won the Irish Sweepstakes. Pop was a steam-fitter, Johnny loaded crates on the docks, and Tim was going to night school. Pop split the million with his two sons. They all vowed the money wouldn't change their plans in life.

A year later, the million wasn't gone, but it was "bent." The boys weren't speaking to Pop, or to each other. Johnny was pursuing expensive race horses and Tim was chasing expensive women. Both boys were on their way to becoming alcoholics. Mom accused Pop of hiding his money from her. Within two years, all of them faced charges for failing to pay their income taxes.[63]

In both cases, these winners had hoped and prayed for sudden wealth. Both had their prayers answered. And both were wrecked on a dollar sign. The cost of a wealthy lifestyle is far more than can be calculated in dollars and cents.

Let your character or moral disposition he free from love of money—[including] greed, avarice, lust, and craving for earthly possessions—and he satisfied with your present [circumstances and with what you have] . .

HEBREWS 13:5 AMP

BEING AT
PEACE WITH
YOURSELF IS A
DIRECT RESULT
OF FINDING
PEACE WITH
GOD.

In deep despair, William Cowper tried to end his life one morning by swallowing poison. His attempt at suicide failed. He then hired a coach and asked to be driven to the Thames River. He intended to hurl himself over the bridge into the icy waters below, but felt "strangely restrained."

The next morning, still immersed in inner darkness, he tried again to end his life by falling on a sharp knife, but he only succeeded in breaking the blade! In one last desperate attempt, he tried to hang himself, but was found and taken down unconscious, but still alive.

Some time later Cowper picked up a Bible and began to read the Book of Romans. It was there that he finally met the God who could speak peace to the storm in his soul. After many years of following the Lord he wrote:

God moves in a mysterious way
His wonders to perform;
He plants His footsteps in the sea,
And rides upon the storm.
Deep in unfathomable mines
Of never-failing skill
He treasures up His bright designs
And works His sovereign will.[64]

Ask the Lord to speak peace to your troubled heart today. He alone is the author of a peace that holds firm.

And the peace of God, which passeth all understanding, shall keep your hearts and minds through Christ Jesus.

PHILIPPIANS 4:7

IF YOU WANT
TO MAKE AN
EASY JOB
SEEM MIGHTY
HARD JUST
KEEP PUTTING
OFF DOING IT.

A teacher once gave his class this assign-ment: "This week, go to someone you love whom you have never, or have not in a long time, said I love you to and tell them you love them."

The next week, he asked if anyone wanted to share what had happened. One student rose and said, "Five years ago, my father and I had a vicious argument and never really resolved it. We avoided each other as much as possible. Once I made the decision to tell him I loved him, however, it was as if a heavy load lifted from my chest. When I told my wife what I was going to do, she didn't just get out of bed, she catapulted out and hugged me. We stayed up half the night talking. It was great!

"The next morning I got to the office two hours early and got more done than most days. After work, I went to see Dad. When he answered the door, I didn't waste any time. I took one step in the door and said, 'Dad, I just came over to tell you that I love you.' His face softened and he began to cry. He reached out and hugged me and said, 'I love you too, son, but I've never been able to say it.'

"Two days later my dad had a heart attack. He's still unconscious and I don't know if he'll make it. The lesson I learned is this, Don't wait to do the things you know need to be done. *Do them now.*"[65]

How long are ye slack to go to possess the land, which the Lord God of your fathers hath given you?

JOSHUA 18:3

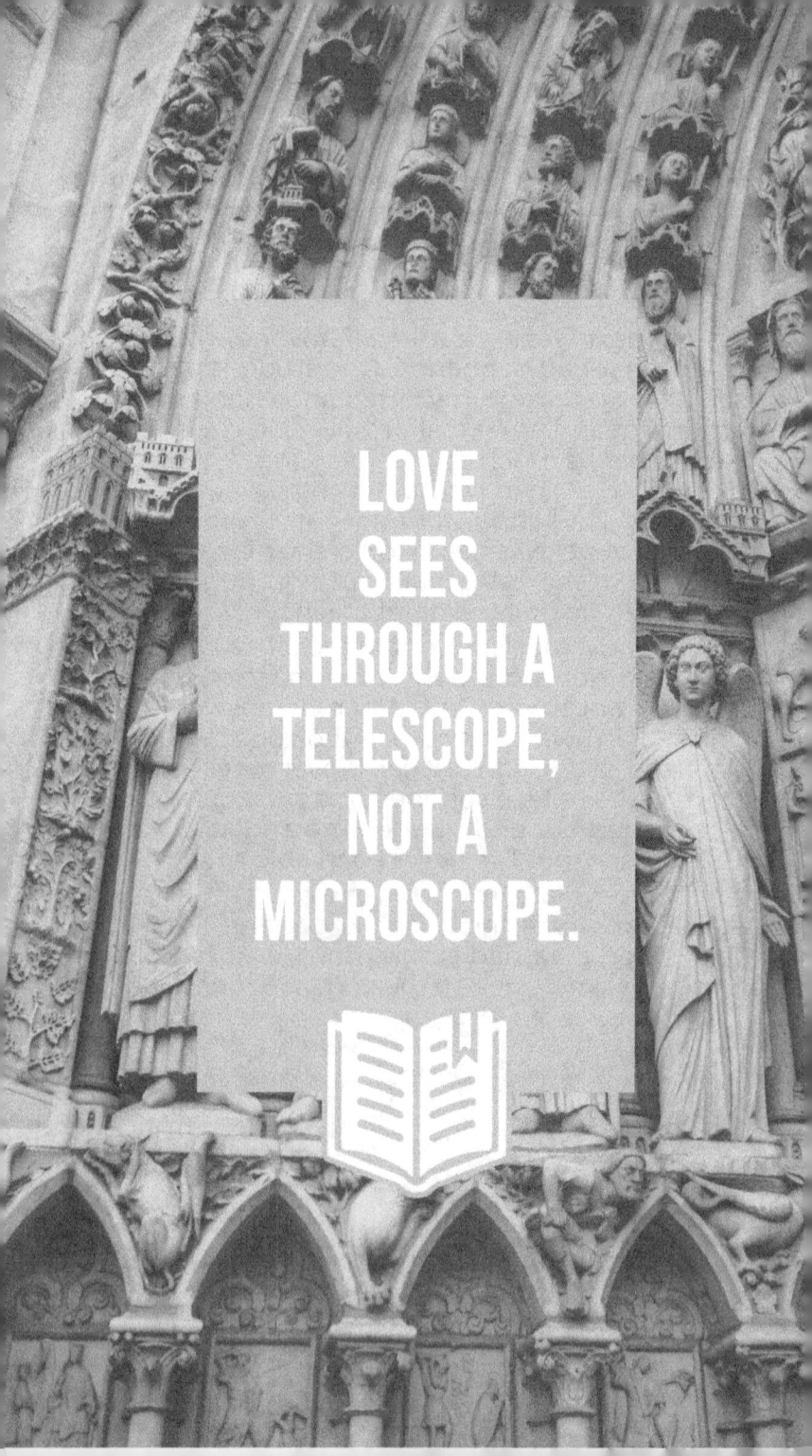

LOVE
SEES
THROUGH A
TELESCOPE,
NOT A
MICROSCOPE.

J an Pitt-Watson has adapted this portion from *A Primer for Preachers*: "There is a natural, logical kind of loving that loves lovely things and lovely people. That's logical. But there is another kind of loving that doesn't look for value in what it loves, but that 'creates' value in what it loves. Like Rosemary's rag doll.

"When Rosemary, my youngest child, was three, she was given a little rag doll, which quickly became an inseparable companion. She had other toys that were intrinsically far more valuable, but none that she loved like she loved the rag doll. Soon the rag doll became more and more rag and less and less doll. It also became more and more dirty. If you tried to clean the rag doll, it became more ragged still. And if you didn't try to clean the rag doll, it became dirtier still.

"The sensible thing to do was to trash the rag doll. But that was unthinkable for anyone who loved my child. If you loved Rosemary, you loved the rag doll—it was part of the package . . . 'Love me, love my rag dolls,' says God, 'including the one you see when you look in the mirror. This is the finest and greatest commandment.'"[66]

Love endures long and is patient and kind . . . it takes no account of the evil done to it [it pays no attention to a suffered wrong.]

1 CORINTHIANS 13:4,5 AMP

LIFE IS NOT A PROBLEM TO BE SOLVED, BUT A GIFT TO BE ENJOYED.

Denis Waitley writes in *The New Dynamics of Winning*, "In 1979, I was booked on a flight from Chicago to Los Angeles. I was on my way to a speaking engagement before going home for the weekend. I had to run for the plane, and became very upset when I saw the gate agent lock the door and then saw the mobile ramp pull away from the plane. I argued and begged and told her I had to be on that nonstop DC 10, Flight 191 to L.A., or I would miss my speech. The plane taxied away from the ramp and out toward the runway despite my protests. I stormed out of the boarding area and back to the ticket counter to register my complaint.

"Standing in line at the counter, about twenty minutes later, I heard the news that the plane had crashed on takeoff with no survivors. I left the ticket line, booked a room at the airport hotel, knelt down beside my bed in prayer, and tried to get some sleep. It's been over a decade since then, but I still have my unvalidated ticket for Flight 191. I never turned it in to my travel agent for a refund. Instead, I tacked it on a bulletin board in my office at home as a silent reminder. About once a year I get a little annoyed with some injustice in the world that has made me a victim . . . My wife, Susan, gently takes me by the hand to my bulletin board."[67]

This is the day which the Lord hath made; we will rejoice and be glad in it.

PSALM 118:24

AS I GROW
OLDER,
I PAY LESS
ATTENTION TO
WHAT MEN SAY.
I JUST WATCH
WHAT THEY DO.

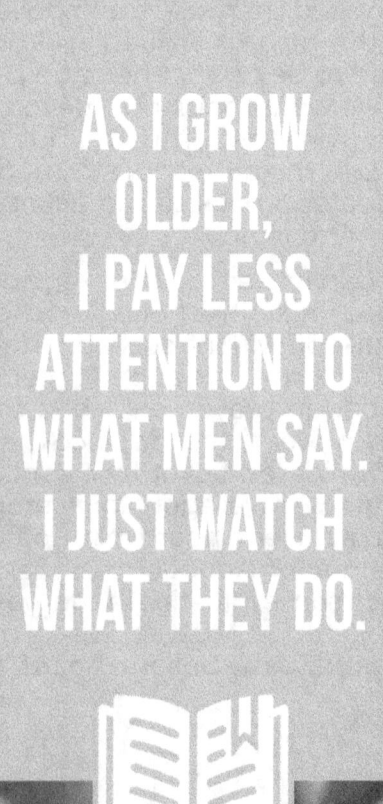

The story is told of a missionary who was lost at sea and by chance, washed up on an island near a remote native village. Finding him half-dead from starvation and exposure, the people of the village nursed him back to health. Fie subsequently lived among the people for some twenty years. During that time he confessed no faith, sang no gospel songs, preached no sermons. He neither read nor recited Scripture and made no claim of personal faith.

However, when the people were sick, he attended them. When they were hungry, he gave them food. When they were lonely, he kept them company. He taught the ignorant, and came to the aid of those who were wronged.

One day missionaries came to the village and began talking to the people about a man called Jesus. After hearing what they had to say of Jesus' ministry and teachings, they insisted that He had been living among them for twenty years. "Come, we will introduce you to the man about whom you have been speaking." They led the missionaries to a hut where they found a long-lost friend, the missionary, whom all had thought dead.[68]

Your true witness for Christ is the sum of all you do, not just what you say.

Show me your faith without deeds, and I will show you my faith by what I do.

JAMES 2:18 NIV

SOME PEOPLE
REACH THE TOP
OF THE LADDER
OF SUCCESS
ONLY TO FIND IT
IS LEANING
AGAINST THE
WRONG WALL.

Two friends landed in New York City, and finding that they had a nine-hour layover between flights, decided to hire a taxi to drive them around so they might see some of the city's famous landmarks. The driver took them to various noteworthy places, taking time to tell the significance of each.

One of the friends was eager to take in all that he could see and hear. He noticed, however, that his friend seemed a bit oblivious to the sights. Instead, his eyes were firmly fixed upon the driver. Finally he whispered to his friend, "Look, he has his sweater on inside out."

Many a person has been known to major on the minors, or to pursue something that is of little significance once it is attained.

A dog once chased a freight train, but when he had succeeded in stopping the train he didn't know what to do with it. In the end, "catching" the train did not bring near the reward he had thought it would. He would have been much more fulfilled as a dog if he had gone after a cat or a rabbit.[69]

Today, make sure that what you are pursuing is truly what you want, should you attain it. Every success has some degree of difficulty. Be certain you can endure the trials without compromising your values or identity.

"But seek ye first the kingdom of God, and his righteousness; and all these things shall be added unto you."

MATTHEW 6:33

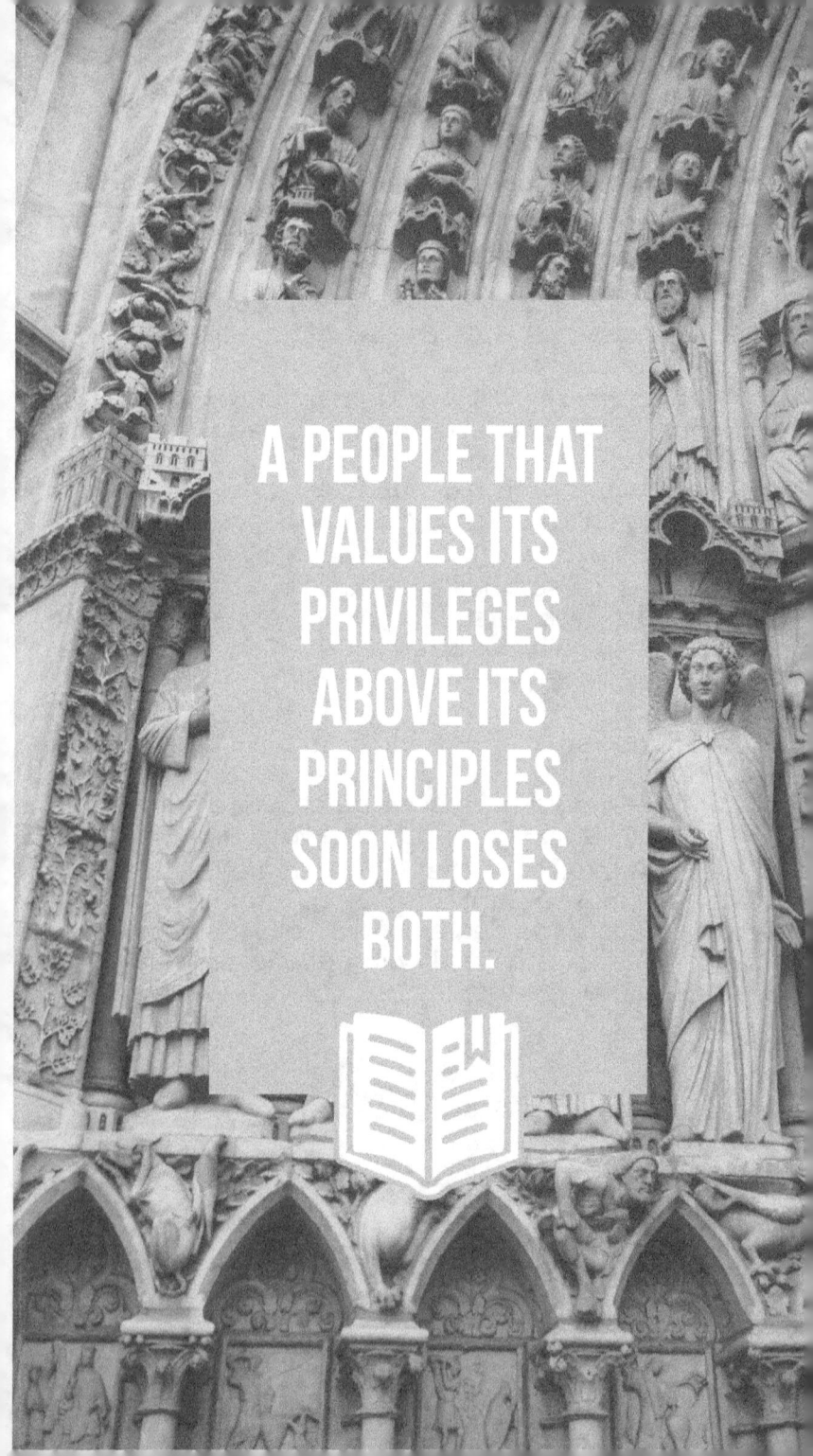

A PEOPLE THAT VALUES ITS PRIVILEGES ABOVE ITS PRINCIPLES SOON LOSES BOTH.

In the 1930s, England had become permeated with pacifism. Millions of soldiers had been lost to the gas warfare and dank trenches of World War I. In reaction, those on both the left and right of the political spectrum showed great support for appeasement and concessions to Hitler.

The Oxford Union Debating Society overwhelmingly approved a resolution that it would "in no circumstances fight for king and country." A pledge, known as the Oxford Oath, was taken by students and teachers across the nation using the same language. The Cambridge Union voted 213 to 138 for "uncompromising" pacifism. The nation was increasingly dispirited and isolated. Meanwhile, Hitler's Nazi tyranny advanced. Whispers of surrender to Hitler began to circulate throughout England.

It was upon this stage that Winston Churchill arose. As one historian has said, he imposed his "imagination and his will upon his countrymen," idealizing them "with such intensity that in the end they approached his ideal and began to see themselves as he saw them." In doing so, "he transformed cowards into brave men, and so fulfilled the purpose of shining armour." Churchill led a nation that had pledged to never fight again, to once again fight and die for king and country.[70]

We must always remember, to whom much is given, much is required.

Uprightness and right standing with God [moral and spiritual rectitude in every area and relation] these elevate a nation, but sin is a reproach to any people.

PROVERBS 14:34 AMP

A PINT OF EXAMPLE IS WORTH A BARRELFUL OF ADVICE.

Entrepreneur and public speaker Wilson Harrell has recalled his best teacher this way: "When I was eleven, my father made me a cotton buyer at his gin. Now I knew cotton, but I was well aware that my father was entrusting an eleven-year-old with an awesome responsibility. When I cut a bale, I pulled out a wad, examined the sample, identified the grade and set the price. I'll never forget the first farmer I faced. He looked at me, called my father over and said, 'Elias, I've worked too hard to have an eleven-year-old boy decide what I'll live on next year.'

"My father was a man of few words. 'His grade stands,' he answered and walked away. Over the years my father never publicly changed my grade. However, when we were alone, he'd check my work. If I'd under-graded (and paid too little), I'd have to go tell the farmer I'd made a mistake and pay him the difference. If I'd over-graded, my father wouldn't say a word—he'd just look at me . . .

"I'm not sure my father knew anything about entrepreneurship, but he understood an awful lot about making a man out of a boy. He gave me responsibility and then backed my hand. He also taught me that fairness builds a business and that the willingness to admit and correct mistakes is a sure way to bring customers back."[71]

When you do what is right, there's not much you have to say.

Brethren, join in following my example, and observe those who walk according to the pattern you have in us.

PHILIPPIANS 3:17 NASB

IT HAS BEEN MY
OBSERVATION
THAT MOST
PEOPLE GET
AHEAD DURING
THE TIME THAT
OTHERS WASTE.

Colonel Rahl, the Hessian commander at Trenton, was in the midst of a game of cards when a courier brought a message to him.

Rahl casually put the letter in his pocket and did not read it until the game was finished. The message was that Washington was crossing the Delaware River. He quickly moved to rally his men, but he was too late. He died just before his regiment was taken captive. Because of a few moments of delay, he lost honor, liberty, and life![72]

There is an old saying, "Tomorrow is the devil's motto." The world's history has born it out as true.

Many a success has been aborted because of half-finished plans and unexecuted resolutions.

In evaluating your immediate future, as well as your ultimate goals, ask yourself these questions:

1. What am I *truly* doing (or planning to do)? Analyze your own actions and motivations thoroughly.

2. Is it what God requires of me? Given the talents, traits, experiences, and abilities He has given me, does it seem likely that this is what God has prepared for me to do, and desires that I accomplish for His sake?

If your answer to these questions is "no," then reevaluate number one. If your answer is "yes," then do what you know to do with as much energy and enthusiasm as possible!

The plans of the diligent lead to profit as surely as haste leads to poverty.

PROVERBS 21:5 NIV

FEAR MAKES THE WOLF BIGGER THAN HE IS.

Eleanor Roosevelt is often described as a woman of great strength, courage, and conviction. She has stated that early in her life, however, she was afraid of everything. She once wrote, "I can remember vividly an occasion when I was living in my grandmother's house on Thirty-seventh Street in New York City. One of my aunts was ill and asked for some ice, which was kept in the icebox out-of-doors in the back yard.

"I was so frightened that I shook. But I could not refuse to go. If I did that, she would never again ask me to help her and I could not bear not to be asked.

"I had to go down alone from the third floor in the dark, creeping through the big house, which was so hostile and unfamiliar at night, in which unknown tenors seemed to lurk. Down to the basement, shutting a door behind me that cut me off from the house and safety. Out in the blackness of the back yard.

"I suffered agonies of fear that night. But I learned that I could face the dark and it never again held such horror for me."[73]

If you want to accomplish anything of merit or lasting value in life, you will have to face down your fears—including the fear of failure.

Though a mighty army marches against me, my heart shall know no fear! I am confident that God will save me.

PSALM 27:3 TLB

BEWARE LEST YOUR FOOTPRINTS ON THE SANDS OF TIME LEAVE ONLY THE MARKS OF A HEEL.

A rather unsavory character was being buried one day. He had never been anywhere near a place of worship his entire life and the services were being conducted by a minister who had never heard of him.

Even so, the minister became carried away with the occasion. He poured on great praise for the departed man in his desire to bring as much comfort as possible to the family.

As the preacher lamented the great loss of this father, husband, and boss, the man's widow—whose expression had grown more and more puzzled—nudged her son and whispered, "Go up there and make sure it's Papa."[74]

Regardless of our station in life or the material possessions we may amass, we will each leave behind an intangible inheritance to future generations. We will either leave a legacy of love, morality, and faith in Christ, or a legacy of hate, immorality, and faithlessness.

Which legacy are you building today?

The memory of the righteous will be a blessing, but the name of the wicked will rot.

PROVERBS 10:7 NIV

THE HAPPINESS OF EVERY COUNTRY DEPENDS UPON THE CHARACTER OF ITS PEOPLE, RATHER THAN THE FORM OF ITS GOVERNMENT.

At the close of the American War of Independence, colonial representatives met to draw up a constitution for their new nation. They talked for several weeks but made little headway toward a consensus. Then, Benjamin Franklin, the representative from Pennsylvania, addressed the assembly. At age eighty-two, he had the admiration of most of those present as a loyal American and a senior statesman.

Franklin told them how during the dark days of the war, he had often gone into the very chamber where they were meeting, to pray. Again and again, he had seen the colonists delivered from sure defeat.

He said, "If not a sparrow can fall to the ground without your heavenly Father, I am sure that no Empire worth rearing can ever be raised without Him." On this note, he suggested that they couch their daily deliberations in prayer. Daily prayer sessions were held thereafter, and the Constitution of the United States was soon drafted, and subsequently adopted.[75]

When you know you are obeying God's commandments and following His directives, you can endure most any circumstance, tackle most any problem, and face most any enemy—including government oppression.

Happy is that people . . . whose God is the Lord.

PSALM 144:15

IN LOVE,
WE MAY FIND IT
BETTER TO
MAKE
ALLOWANCES,
RATHER THAN
MAKE POINTS.

During a marriage counseling session, a wife's foremost complaint was that her husband treated other people better than he treated her. "A perfect example happened the other night," she said. "When we finished dinner at Elaine's house, you got up from the table, helped clear all the dishes, and then offered to rinse them. Elaine said to me later, 'Larry certainly is a wonderful husband. I hope you know how fortunate you are.' It hurt me to see you go out of your way to help someone else, but you wouldn't do those things for me. You were considerate of Elaine's needs and not of mine."

Larry asked, "How did you answer Elaine when she said that about me?"

His wife answered, "I felt like telling her what I really thought. *This is a nice show, but he never does it when he's home.* But I didn't. I just said, 'Larry's a great guy.'"

"Why?" Larry asked. "Why didn't you tell her what you really thought?"

She replied, "I wasn't going to be disloyal to you. Why would I say something bad about you? I want to work things out in our marriage—why would I criticize you and drive yet another wedge between us in my heart?"[76]

Hate always divides, even if that hate is harbored only within one's heart and never spoken. In contrast, a heart filled with love binds people together.

Above all, love each other deeply because love covers a multitude of sins.

1 PETER 4:8 NIV

STANDING IN THE
MIDDLE OF THE
ROAD IS VERY
DANGEROUS:
YOU GET KNOCKED
DOWN BY THE
TRAFFIC FROM
BOTH SIDES.

As a boy, Steven was ambivalent about his Jewish heritage. To him, being Jewish often meant not being part of the "normal" world. Christmastime was especially tough since he lived on a block that won awards for its Christmas decorations, with the exception of his home, which he dubbed "the black hole."

His sense of being different was heightened when his family moved to a Phoenix neighborhood with very few Jews. Then, when his father took a job in northern California, he experienced his first overt anti-Semitism. His high-school peers openly ridiculed him, and one bully routinely hit him during flag football games.

When Steven's first child, Max, was born, he said, "I thought about the beliefs my parents had tried to instill in me when I was young and unwilling to listen." Although he believed other film makers were better suited for the project, Steven Spielberg proudly embraced his Jewish heritage and made the film, *Schindler's List*.

During the filming he realized, "As a Jew, if I had been in this spot fifty years ago, I would have received an automatic death sentence . . . There were evenings when I'd come home from shooting and just need to be held by my wife." In coming to grips with his roots, however, Spielberg fulfilled himself both artistically and personally.[77]

God has created each one of us with unique gifts and talents that can be expressed by no one else. Express your *real* self today—without compromise.

I know thy works, that thou art neither cold nor hot: I would thou wert cold or hot.

REVELATION 3:15

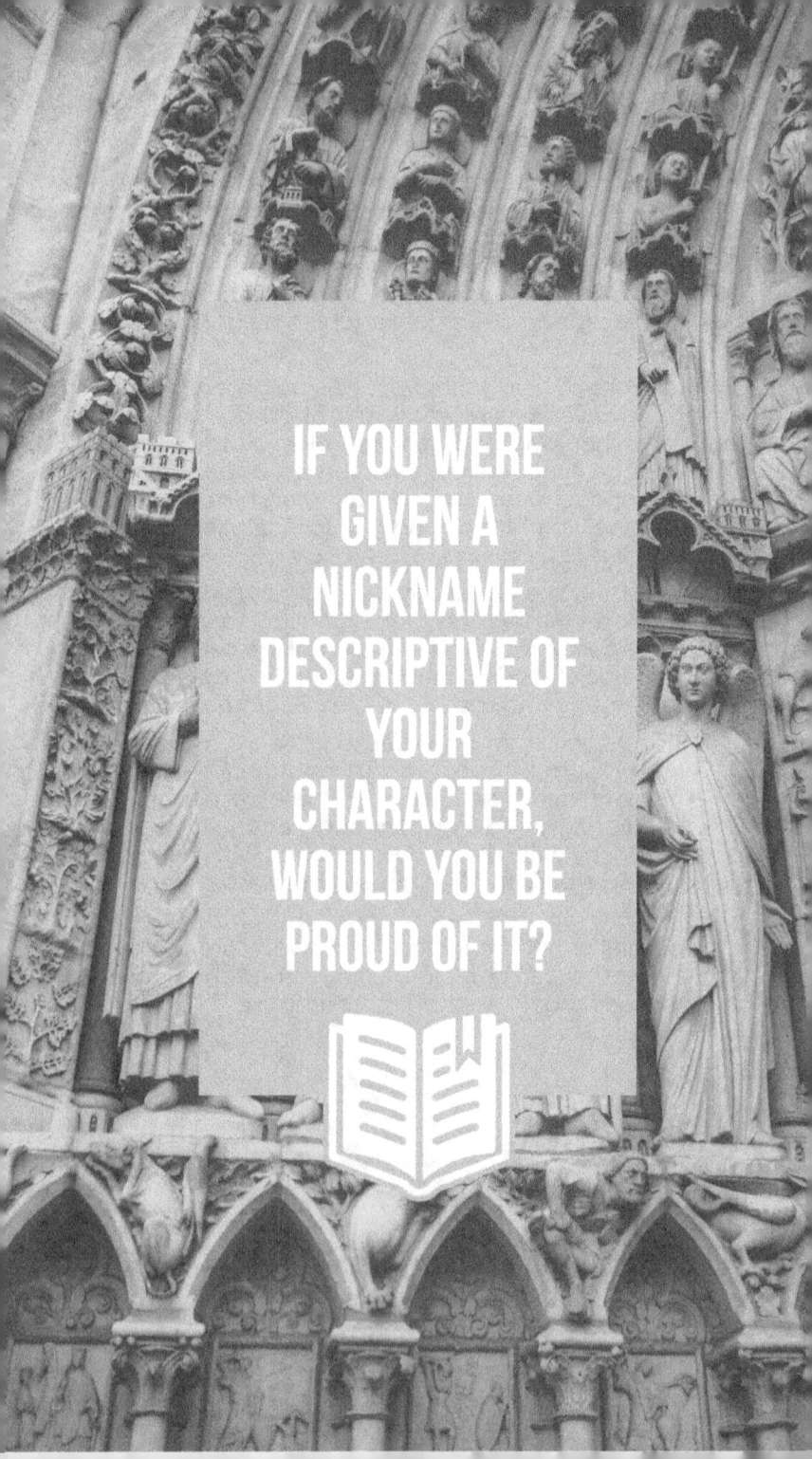

IF YOU WERE GIVEN A NICKNAME DESCRIPTIVE OF YOUR CHARACTER, WOULD YOU BE PROUD OF IT?

John Selwyn, who became the Bishop of the South Pacific, was renowned for his boxing skill during his university days. On one occasion after he had become bishop, he had to utter grave words of warning and rebuke to a professed convert. The man clenched his fist and violently struck the bishop on the face.

In response, Selwyn simply folded his arms and looked into the man's face. With his powerful arm and massive fist he could easily have knocked the man down, but instead he waited calmly for another blow. It was too much for his assailant. Ashamed, he fled into the jungle.

Years later, the bishop become seriously ill, so he returned home. One day, the man who had struck him came to his successor to confess Christ in baptism. Convinced of the genuineness of his conversion, the new bishop asked what "new name" he desired to take as a Christian. "Call me John Selwyn," the man replied, "for it was he who taught me what Jesus Christ is like."[78]

Do others call you a Christian, or is that only what you call yourself? If not the name of Christ, what name do your friends give you behind your back?

A good name is rather to be chosen than great riches.

PROVERBS 22:1

IT'S EASY TO
IDENTIFY PEOPLE
WHO CAN'T COUNT
TO TEN.
THEY'RE IN FRONT
OF YOU IN THE
SUPERMARKET
EXPRESS LANE.

Sundays were very important to Peggy, a working single mother. Worshipping God refreshed her spirit and her mind. Fellowship with other church members gave her support and encouragement. However, the hassles of prodding a slow-moving teenage daughter to get ready for church often took their toll on her patience.

Running late one Sunday morning, Peggy got stuck on the freeway behind an elderly couple moving well below the speed limit. Her frustration mounted with each passing mile. "Why do people so old even get on the freeway? Why can't they speed up? They're making me late to church!" she yelled, her daughter being her only audience.

Finally, an opening in the next lane allowed her to slip past the older couple. She looked over at them as she passed, ready to give them an angry glare and discovered that the driver of the car was her beloved pastor![79]

How many times are we quick to judge, even quick to respond in anger, only to discover that it is our own motives and attitudes that are in need of judgment!

Be patient with everyone.

1 THESSALONIANS 5:14 NIV

TACT IS THE
ART OF
MAKING A
POINT
WITHOUT
MAKING AN
ENEMY.

D ianne Hales has offered these guidelines for tactfully confronting someone about undesirable behavior:

1. *Do no harm.* Before blurting out any sordid truth, gauge whether or not your friend is ready to hear it. Ask yourself what you hope to accomplish by getting involved. Says one family counselor, "It's always a good idea to knock before entering another person's psyche."

2. *Be sensitive, not superior.* Choose the time and place wisely. Never set another person up for embarrassment. Sandwich your comments between compliments.

3. *Keep your emotions in check.* Think twice before popping off in anger.

4. *"Seed" the unconscious.* Depersonalize the issue. Describe a parallel situation as a mirror for the person. Express your concerns using "I" statements, not accusatory "you" statements.

5. *Be brief.* Get to the point quickly, then say no more. Give the person time to recover and respond.[80]

Always ask yourself, do you want to bash the person, or help him? If your motive truly is to help, you'll find a way to speak the truth with love.

Reckless words pierce like a sword, but the tongue of the wise brings healing.

PROVERBS 12:18 NIV

BE CAREFUL OF YOUR THOUGHTS: THEY MAY BECOME WORDS AT ANY MOMENT.

One day, St. Francis of Assisi said to several of his followers: "Let us go to the village over the way and preach." As they went, they met a man who was greatly burdened in his spirit. Francis was in no hurry, so he stopped and listened attentively to the man's tale of woe.

Upon reaching the village, Francis talked with the shopkeepers, spent time with the farmers at their vegetable and fruit stalls, and played with the children in the streets. On the way back to the monastery, he and his followers were met by a farmer with a load of hay. Francis stopped to talk with him. By the time he said good-bye, the morning was gone.

One of the followers seemed disappointed. He said to Francis, "Brother Francis, you said you were going to preach. The morning is spent and no sermon has been given."

The saintly Francis replied, "But we have been preaching all the way."[81]

Not only do our thoughts give rise to words, but to actions. As we think, so we speak and do. As we act, so we are. Choose, therefore, with great care what you will think. In your thoughts are the seeds of your reputation.

A wise man's heart guides his mouth.

PROVERBS 16:23 NIV

FANATIC:
A PERSON WHO'S
ENTHUSIASTIC
ABOUT
SOMETHING IN
WHICH YOU HAVE
NO INTEREST.

Kidnapped by pirates as a teenager, Patrick was taken from his well-to-do home in Roman Britain in 405 A.D., transported to Ireland, sold to a farmer, and given responsibility for the man's sheep. Patrick had grown up in a Christian home. However, his faith did not become real to him until one day, while tending sheep in the barren hills of Ireland, he encountered the Great Shepherd and committed his life to Him.

Patrick eventually escaped from slavery and returned to Britain, where he became a priest. Then in a dream, he heard an Irish voice pleading with him, "Holy boy, we are asking you to come home and walk among us again." To return to the land of his servitude? It was an unlikely mission, but Patrick now saw himself as a slave to Christ. The Lord gave him a compassion for the Irish. He later wrote, "I was struck to the heart."

Patrick returned to Ireland to take the Gospel to those enslaved by superstition and Druid worship. He baptized thousands of converts, discipled new believers, trained church leaders, ordained pastors, disciplined unrepentant church members, commissioned evangelists, and started scores of churches.[82]

To some, Patrick was a fanatic. To those to whom he brought the message of Christ, he was and remains Saint Patrick.

Never be lacking in zeal, but keep your spiritual fervor, serving the Lord.

ROMANS 12:11 NIV

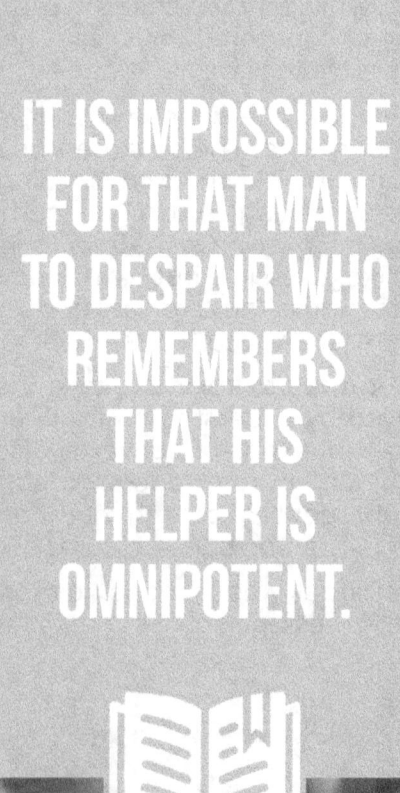

IT IS IMPOSSIBLE
FOR THAT MAN
TO DESPAIR WHO
REMEMBERS
THAT HIS
HELPER IS
OMNIPOTENT.

D r. Joseph Leroy Dodds once wrote to his granddaughter: "A common greeting of these days is, 'How are you?' The stereotype reply is, 'Fine, and how are you?' I frequently give this reply to my friends who would be dismayed and bored if I tried to tell them the truth, for the edition of this jalopy which I call my body is getting worse and worse . . .

"The steering gear is so worn and wobbly that I have to use a cane to keep it from running off the road. The headlights are so dim that they show up only about half or a third as much as they used to. The horn is a mere squawk. I only get about a tenth of the speed out of it that it gave a few years ago. And as for climbing hills, or even gentler slopes, the less said the better . . .

"But the real person who lives inside this jalopy is a different story. God is much more real and His truth shines more brightly. The companionship of Christ is more constant through His Holy Spirit, and He holds out a hope for a new model, after this jalopy is junked . . .

"I know I do not deserve a new model, and if God, the righteous Judge, determines that I should not have it, that is all right, too. In any case, Righteous Judge is His middle name, sandwiched between His first and last names, both of which are *love*. So, I am fine, thank you. How are you?"[83]

I lift up my eyes to the hills—where does my help come from? My help comes from the Lord . . . The Lord will keep you from all harm—he will watch over your life.

PSALM 121:1,2,7 NIV

SILENCE IS
ONE OF THE
HARDEST
ARGUMENTS
TO REFUTE.

While in the midst of contending with the many geographic problems encountered while building the Panama Canal, Colonel George Washington Goethals had to endure a great deal of criticism from those back home who predicted he would never complete his great task. The visionary builder continued on, seeming to ignore their carping. "Aren't you going to answer your critics?" some asked.

"In time," Goethals replied.

"How?" they asked.

The engineer smiled and said simply, "With the canal."

Ole Bull, a violinist in the nineteenth century, was once offered space in the *New York Herald* to answer his critics. He said, "I think it is best that they write against me and I play against them."

The finest argument against one's detractors is faithfully doing the very best one can do—consistently, persistently, and insistently. Diligent performance disarms criticism. It wins sympathy. It wastes no time and suffers no loss. As one commentator from Bull's time noted, "Practical doing is ever better than fault-finding or trying to satisfy the censorious. And the world knows it."[84]

Make your steady, faithful work your best defense. It will not only prove your critics wrong, but will stifle their criticism.

Whoso keepeth his mouth and his tongue keepeth his soul from troubles.

PROVERBS 21:23

ANYONE CAN HOLD THE HELM WHEN THE SEA IS CALM.

A s a passenger on the *S.S. Constitution*, Norman Vincent Peale once found himself skirting the edge of a hurricane. He has written, "The ship was bucking like a demented horse. I was lying on my bed in my cabin, thinking pale green thoughts, when the door opened and in came a cheery fellow who had a cabin down the corridor . . . He said, 'Let's go up and look at the storm.'"

When Peale protested and asked the man to leave, the man took out a booklet and read him a passage about the importance of taking authority over weaknesses and fears. Peale wasn't all that impressed but asked, "Who wrote it?"

The man replied, "You did."

Shamed into going up on deck, Peale writes, "Mountainous waves came racing at us like avalanches, the wind ripping the spray off their crests like smoke. Great streamers of spume lashed our faces and soaked our clothes. I could taste the salt on my lips. The deck heaved, the gale shrieked in our ears, but the ship was more than equal to it . . . I was lost in admiration . . . of nature's power and fury, and the courage and ingenuity of the puny creature called man who had built this ship and could drive it through the teeth of such a storm." His seasickness completely disappeared.[85]

Get your mind off yourself and onto God. He not only calms stormy seas but gives us courage to ride the waves.

If thou faint in the day of adversity, thy strength is small.

PROVERBS 24:10

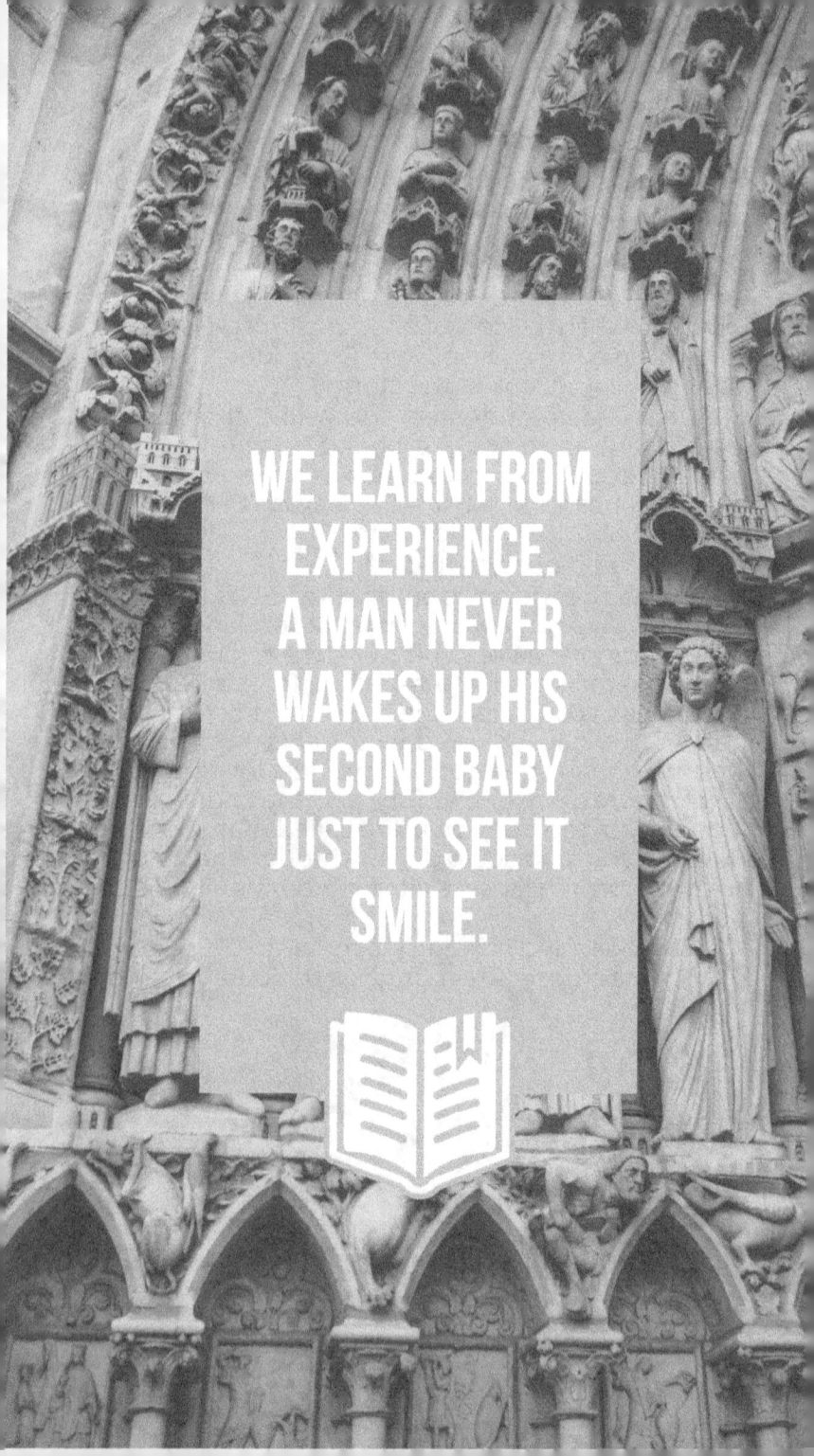

WE LEARN FROM
EXPERIENCE.
A MAN NEVER
WAKES UP HIS
SECOND BABY
JUST TO SEE IT
SMILE.

During her senior year of high school, Lynn became ill with bronchitis and missed two weeks of school. She returned to school to discover she had nine tests to make up in one week! When she got to the last test, she drew a total blank. She admitted to her teacher, "I can't do this. I don't know any of these answers."

He went over to her, and looking at her paper said, "You know the answer to that! We just talked about it in class yesterday. You answered a question I asked about that."

In spite of several hints, she just could not remember. She said, "You're just gonna have to give me an *F*. I can't do it. I feel too bad." He reached down with his red pencil and as she watched, certain he was going to put an *F* on the paper, he wrote a big, bold *A* at the top of the page.

"What are you doing?" she asked.

He said, "If you had been here and you felt good and you'd had time to study, that's what you would have earned. So that's what you are going to get."

Lynn reflected later, "I realized there are people who will give you a break once in a while. It was empowering. It was like he was saying, 'I know who you are, not just what you do.' That's an amazing gift to give somebody. That's the kind of teacher I want to be."[86]

We should always take into consideration the whole of who a person is, not just the mistake or blunder he or she may have made most recently.

> The things you have learned and received and heard and seen in me, practice these things; and the God of peace shall be with you.
>
> PHILIPPIANS 4:9 NASB

THE BEST ANTIQUE IS AN OLD FRIEND.

Friendship is something we often take for granted. Then, if a friend moves away or dies, we are reminded that friendship must be consistently nurtured. Friendship thrives on frequent encounters, meaningful exchanges, and the shared secrets.

I would rather have the sunshine
Of your pleasant smile today,
Than to have on some tomorrow
A belated, grand banquet.

I would rather have the pleasure
Of your happy presence now,
Than to wait until tomorrow
For some stilted pledge or vow.

I would rather walk with you awhile
Today in some friendly mode,
Than to wait until tomorrow comes
To drive along the road.

I'd rather be the present friend
In every gentle way,
So let us make the most of it
While it is called today.[87]

E. J. MORGAN

Today, take time to be a "present friend" who expresses friendship in a "gentle way."

Your own friend and your father's friend, forsake them not . . . Better is a neighbor who is near [in spirit] than a brother who is far off [in heart].

PROVERBS 27:10 AMP

PRAY AS IF
EVERYTHING
DEPENDED ON
GOD,
AND WORK AS IF
EVERYTHING
DEPENDED UPON
MAN.

Years ago, Austin—an inner-city neighborhood in Chicago—was a solid, stable community. But like many urban centers in America after the 1960s, the area experienced "white flight." Property values plunged. Large corporations like Sunbeam and Shell Oil, and many small businesses, moved out—as did a number of churches.

Today, Austin's streets are rife with crack and cocaine. The generals of the local gangs carry submachine guns, make twenty-thousand-dollar drug deals, and routinely kill each other.

Not all of Austin is caught in this mire, however. The Rock of Our Salvation Church and Circle Urban Ministries offer many services to the community: a health clinic, legal clinic, individual and family counseling, food for the hungry, shelters for the homeless, low-rent housing, high-school equivalency education, job training, job placement, and worship opportunities. The leaders of the church and outreach ministries are Raleigh Washington, who is black, and Glen Kehrein, who is white.

In recent years, Circle Urban Ministries has been buying up former crack dens and vacant lots and renovating them into housing. Glen has said, "We're . . . taking back the turf, block by block. We can't buy it all. But we can buy enough so Christians can move in and by their presence preserve the rest of it."[88]

Faith is intended for action.

Faith without works is dead.

JAMES 2:26

A GOOD THING TO REMEMBER, A BETTER THING TO DO— WORK WITH THE CONSTRUCTION GANG, NOT THE WRECKING CREW.

A man once watched his six-year-old son as he built a model airplane. The boy was using a super adhesive glue and in less than three minutes, his right index finger was bonded to a shiny blue wing of his DC-10. He tried desperately to free it. He tugged it, pulled it, and waved it frantically, but it wouldn't budge. The father soon located a solvent that dissolved the glue and the crisis was over.

Some time later, the father visited a new family in the neighborhood. The father of the family introduced his three children:

"This is Pete. He's the clumsy one of the lot."

"That's Kathy coming in with mud on her shoes. She's the sloppy one."

"As always, Mike's last. He'll be late for his own funeral, I promise you."

The father noted, "This man did a thorough job of gluing his children to their faults and mistakes."[89]

Many people feel glued to false guilt and negative self-esteem. Don't contribute to this gluing process in your children or those you love. Rather, be one who bears the solvent of the Gospel, with the message of God's free gift of unconditional love, forgiveness, and spiritual freedom for all who will turn to Him.

When you meet together, each one has a hymn, a teaching, a disclosure of special knowledge or information, an utterance in a [strange] tongue, or an interpretation of it. [But] let everything be constructive and edifying and for the good of all.

1 CORINTHIANS 14:26 AMP

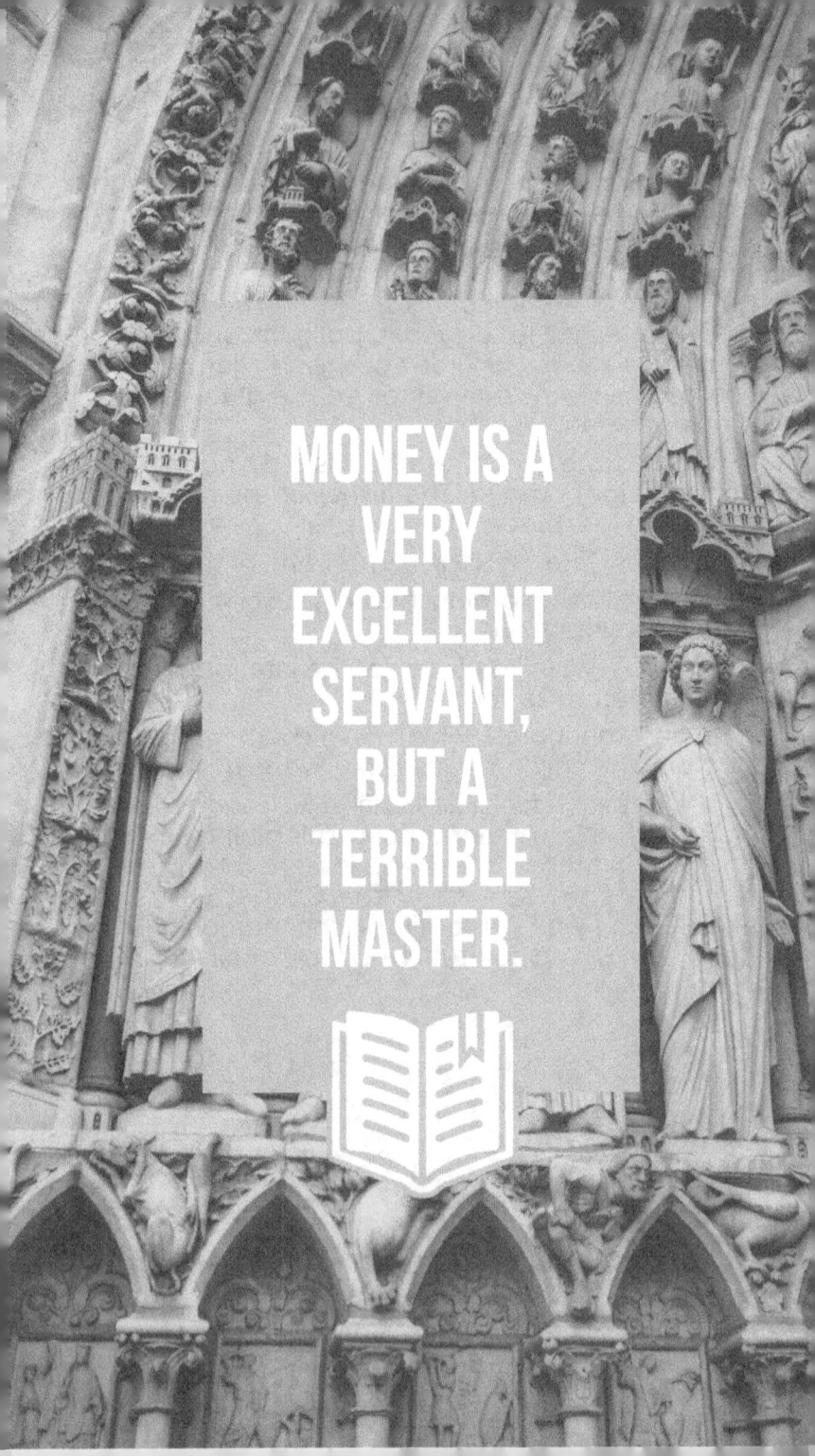

MONEY IS A VERY EXCELLENT SERVANT, BUT A TERRIBLE MASTER.

In the aftermath of the sinking of the ill-fated *Titanic*, reports noted that eleven million-aires had been among the hundreds on board who went to a watery grave in April 1912. Their combined wealth totaled nearly $200,000,000. Yet if these millionaires could have sent a message to the living about the most important things in life, not one would have mentioned money.

Newspapers also reported that Major A. H. Peuchen of Toronto, who was a survivor of the tragedy, had left more than $300,000 in money, jewelry, and securities in his cabin. He started back for the box when evacuation efforts began, but then thought an instant and quickly turned away. Later he said, "The money seemed a mockery at that time. I picked up three oranges instead."

Money is intended to serve us, not to rule us. Margeurite Jackson, an Indianapolis widow, was ruled by her wealth. She lived in constant fear that her money would be stolen. When she died, more than five million dollars was found in her home. The money, one report concluded, "had brought Mrs. Jackson nothing but a life of private terror."[90]

How are you regarding money today? Is it a tool, or a crutch? A prison, or a key?

Command those who are rich in this present world not to be arrogant nor to put their hope in wealth, which is so uncertain, but to put their hope in God, who richly provides us with everything for our enjoyment.

1 TIMOTHY 6:17 NIV

IF YOU CAN'T
FEED A
HUNDRED
PEOPLE THEN
JUST FEED
ONE.

Trevor was an average eleven-year-old when he saw a television special on Philadelphia's homeless. As he watched the scenes of men and women huddled in alleys and under bridges, he felt compelled to do something. But what could a boy his age do? The only thing he could think of was to convince his parents to drive him from their well-to-do suburb into the heart of the city and let him give away his own pillow and blanket.

As they drove the streets of the downtown area, Trevor spotted a derelict camped on top of a subway grate. He remembers that he was wearing white socks, but no shoes. Getting out of the car, Trevor walked over and gave him the pillow and blanket. Amazed, the man looked into Trevor's eyes, smiled, and said, "God bless you."

The die was cast. Trevor had created a mission for himself. Two nights later he and his father were on the streets again, this time taking one of Trevor's mother's old coats. He returned again and again, with more old clothes and hot food. When his own family ran out of clothing to give, Trevor began canvassing his neighborhood. Word of his mission soon reached the local television stations, and the flow of gifts quickly became a flood.[91]

Start with one act of kindness and see what God will do.

As we have therefore opportunity, let us do good unto all men.

GALATIANS 6:10

THE TROUBLE
WITH
STRETCHING
THE TRUTH IS
THAT IT'S APT
TO SNAP BACK.

The story is told of an old minister who survived the great Johnstown flood. He loved to tell the story over and over, usually in great detail. Everywhere he went, all he talked about was this great historic event in his life. Eventually, he died and went to heaven.

In heaven, he attended a meeting of saints who had gathered to share their life experiences. The old minister was very excited. He ran to ask Peter if he might relate the exciting story of his survival from the Johnstown flood.

Peter hesitated for a moment and then said, "Yes, you may share, but just remember that Noah will be in the audience tonight."[92]

When you tell the tales of your life it is always wise to remember that there may be at least two people hidden somewhere in your audience: someone who was there—an eyewitness, and someone who has had a similar experience, but on a much greater scale. The best course is always to tell your experience as accurately as possible. The same holds for criticism and judgment of others. Both understatements and exaggerations are lies.

A false witness shall not be unpunished, and he that speaketh lies shall not escape.

PROVERBS 19:5

BIRTHDAYS ARE
GOOD FOR YOU.
STATISTICS
SHOW THAT THE
PEOPLE WHO
HAVE THE MOST
LIVE THE
LONGEST.

M any people are familiar with the childhood chorus:

Jesus loves me, this I know,
For the Bible tells me so.
Little ones to Him belong,
They are weak but He is strong.

But are you familiar with the verses that C. D. Frey has written for this tune?

Jesus loves me, this I know,
Though my hair is white as snow;
Though my sight is growing dim,
Still He bids me trust in Him.

Though my steps are, oh, so slow,
With my hands in His I'll go
On through life, let come what may,
He'll be there to lead the way.

When the nights are dark and long,
In my heart He puts a song,
Telling me in words so clear,
"Have no fear for I am near."

When my work on earth is done
And life's victories 'been won
He will take me home above
To the fullness of His love.[93]

The fact is, no matter what your age, Jesus still loves you!

So teach us to number our days, that we may apply our hearts unto wisdom.

PSALM 90:12

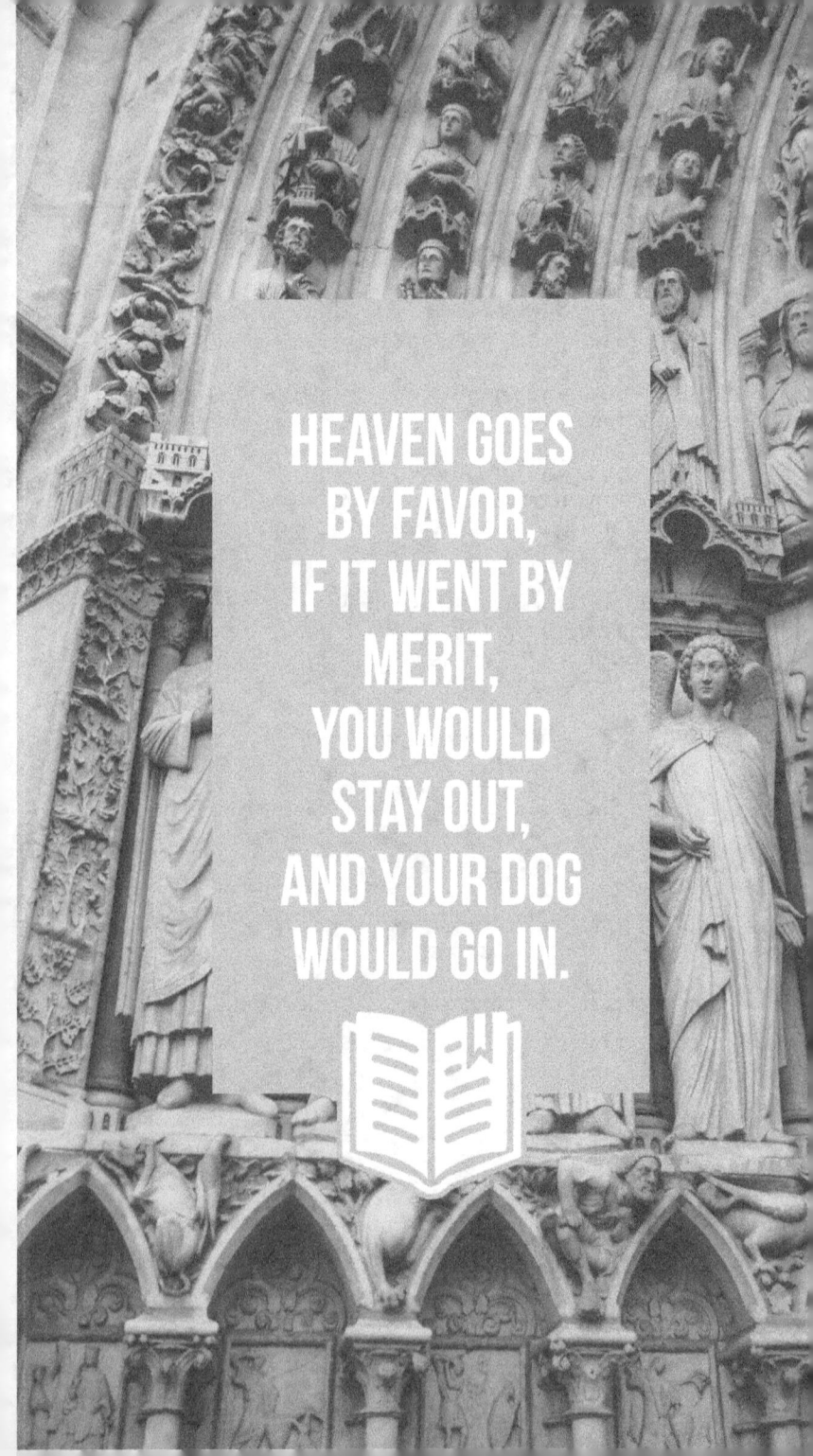

HEAVEN GOES
BY FAVOR,
IF IT WENT BY
MERIT,
YOU WOULD
STAY OUT,
AND YOUR DOG
WOULD GO IN.

Laura Ingalls Wilder writes in *Little House in the Ozarks* about an old dog, Shep, who was learning to sit up and shake hands: "Try as he would, he could not seem to get the knack of keeping his balance in the upright position . . . After a particularly disheartening session one day, we saw him out on the back porch alone and not knowing that he was observed. He was practicing his lesson without a teacher. We watched while he tried and failed several times, then finally got the trick of it and sat up with his paw extended. The next time we said, 'How do you do, Shep?' he had his lesson perfectly.

As he grew older, Shep's eyesight became poor and he didn't always recognize friends. Wilder writes, "Once he made a mistake and barked savagely at an old friend whom he really regarded as one of the family, though he had not seen him for some time. Later, as we all sat in the yard, Shep seemed uneasy . . . At last he walked deliberately to the visitor, sat up, and held out his paw. It was so plainly an apology that our friend said, 'That's all right, Shep, old fellow! Shake and forget it!' Shep shook hands and walked away perfectly satisfied."[94]

Is there an apology you need to make today?

For it is by free grace (God's unmerited favor) that you are saved.

EPHESIANS 2:8 AMP

A BLIND MAN
WHO SEES IS
BETTER THAN
A SEEING MAN
WHO IS BLIND.

A businessman working in the Orient had the occasion to meet a blind man from Belgium who sat next to him during dinner and a show. The man said, "I'd love if you'd describe a little of what you see." The businessman happily agreed.

The blind man asked him to describe the musicians, which the businessman had failed to note, and then to describe their instruments. "What do our fellow tourists look like?" the blind man asked. The businessman described two in detail: an elderly Japanese woman and a blond Scandinavian boy. When the show began, he described the dancers, their golden four-inch fingernails and their elegant movements.

The businessman recalls that as the evening progressed, "I discovered colors, patterns and designs of local costumes, the texture of skin under soft lights, the movement of long, black Asian hair as elegant heads angled to the music, the intense expressions of the musicians as they played, even the flashing white smile of our waitress." At the close of the evening, the blind man said, "How beautifully you saw everything for me."

The businessman later reflected, "I should have thanked him. I was the one who had been blind. He had helped me lift the veil that grows so quickly over our eyes in this hectic world, and to see all those things I'd failed to marvel at before."[95]

"But blessed are your eyes, for they see: and your ears, for they hear."

MATTHEW 13:16

IF THE ROOTS ARE DEEP AND STRONG THE TREE NEEDN'T WORRY ABOUT THE WIND.

C onsider these facts about trees and roots:
  · Forestry experts have estimated that the root spread of many trees is equal to the spread of their branches.

 · In general, as much as one-tenth of a tree is concealed in its roots.

 · The combined length of the roots of a large oak tree would total several hundred miles.

 · The giant saguaro tree of the southwest desert spreads its roots as much as forty or fifty feet underground laterally from the trunk.

 · Hair-like as some tree roots are, an entire system of them can still exert tremendous pressure. For example, the roots of a birch tree, though considered a less sturdy tree than many others, can lift a boulder weighing twenty tons.

 · A tree's root system serves two functions: to anchor the tree, and to collect moisture, without which the tree could not thrive.

 · In Herbstein, Germany, town officials require every newly married couple to plant three sapling birches on the "Marriage Road."[96]

A tree's roots adapt to strengthen it against whatever may try to attack it. If it is wind, the roots grow thick and deep. If it is drought, the roots grow toward water.

Our roots have a direct affect on our branches, and therefore, our fruit. Roots grow under the surface, out of sight. It is the inward matters of life, our thoughts and motives, that enable us to produce strength on the outside.

"Blessed is the man who trusts in the Lord . . . He will be like a tree planted by the water that sends out its roots by the stream. It does not fear when heat comes; its leaves are always green. It has no worries in a year of drought and never fails to bear fruit."

JEREMIAH 17:7,8 NIV

MEN OCCASIONALLY STUMBLE OVER THE TRUTH, BUT MOST OF THEM PICK THEMSELVES UP AND HURRY OFF AS IF NOTHING HAPPENED.

In *First Things First*, Stephen R. Covey tells about a talk he gave to a large group of college students on the subject of the "new morality." He could tell as he talked that the students disagreed with his assertion that there are principles in this world that should be respected and adhered to, no matter who you are or how much you believe in personal freedom.

One student presented a case and said there was no right or wrong in that situation; it was a matter of interpretation. Not so, said Covey. Anytime you violate a fundamental principle, there's a price to be paid. By the look on the students' faces, however, Covey knew they considered him to be out of touch with present-day reality.

"Let's try an experiment," Covey suggested. "I believe that each of you knows in your heart what the truth is. Sit quietly for one minute, listen to your heart, and ask yourself what the truth is concerning this situation."

At the end of the minute, Covey asked the young man what he thought now. He admitted that his heart had told him the exact opposite of what he had been saying. Another young man admitted that he wasn't so sure of himself anymore either.[97]

There comes a time when we each need to stop listening to the crowd and pay attention to the still, small voice that speaks inside of us.

The ear that heareth the reproof of life
abideth among the wise.

PROVERBS 15:31

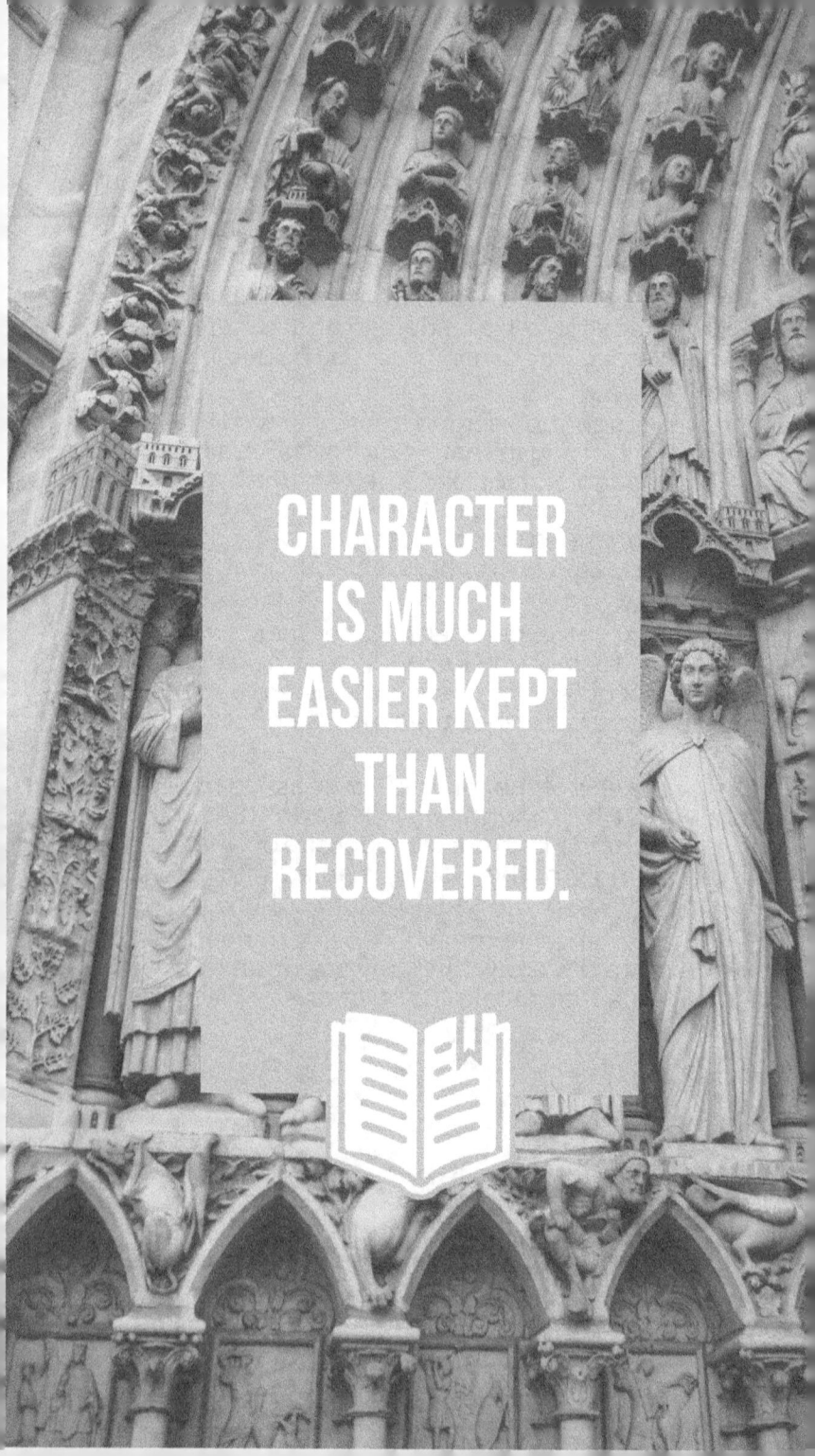

CHARACTER
IS MUCH
EASIER KEPT
THAN
RECOVERED.

In 1994, golfer David Love III called a one-stroke penalty on himself during the second round of the Western Open. He had moved his marker to get it out of another player's putting line. A couple of holes later, he couldn't remember if he had moved his ball back to its original spot. Since he was unsure, he gave himself an extra stroke.

As it turned out, that one stroke caused him to miss the cut and he was eliminated from the tournament. If he had made the cut and then finished dead last, he would have at least earned $2,000 for the week. When the year was over, Love was $590 short in winnings to automatically qualify for the Masters Tournament. Love began 1995 needing to win a tournament to get into the event.

Someone asked Love if it would bother him if he missed the Masters for calling a penalty on himself. Love answered quickly, "How would I feel if I won the Masters and wondered for the rest of my life if I cheated to get in?"

Fortunately, the story has a happy ending. The week before the 1995 Masters, Love qualified by winning a tournament in New Orleans. He finished second in the Master's, earning $237,600.[98]

There are times when it seems costly to preserve one's character. However, it is always more costly to abandon it.

In speech, conduct, love, faith, and purity, show yourself an example of those who believe.

1 TIMOTHY 4:12 NASB

FAULTS ARE
THICK
WHERE LOVE
IS THIN.

According to Aesop's Fables, when Jupiter made man, he gave him two wallets—one for his neighbor's faults, the other for his own. He then threw the wallets over man's shoulders, so that one hung in front and the other in back. The one in front was for his neighbor's faults, and the one in back contained his own. While the neighbor's faults were always under his nose, it took considerable effort for him to see his own. Aesop concludes: "This custom, which began early, is not quite unknown at the present day." Indeed not.

We often tend to look at our neighbor's errors with a microscope and at our own through the wrong end of a telescope. We have two sets of weights and measures, one for home use, the other for foreign.

The story is told of a family who was on its way home from church. The father was criticizing the sermon, the mother was finding fault with the choir, and the sister was running down the organist. They all quieted down in a hurry, however, when the youngest member of the family piped up from the back seat, "I thought it was a pretty good show for a dime."[99]

Before you say *anything* about another person today, ask yourself, "What might that person say about me?"

And above all things have fervent chanty among yourselves: for charity shall cover the multitude of sins.

1 PETER 4:8

THE ONLY
WAY TO HAVE
A FRIEND IS
TO BE ONE.

Mary Lennox "was not an affectionate child and had never cared much for anyone." And no wonder. Ignored by her parents and raised by servants, she had no concept of what life was like outside of India. Other children called her "Mistress Mary Quite Contrary," because she didn't like to share and always insisted on having her own way.

When Mary was nine years old, her parents died of cholera and she was sent to live at her uncle's home in England. The move did nothing to improve her disposition. She expected anyone and everyone to jump when she snapped her fingers.

Gradually, however, Mary began to change. Realizing how lonely she was, she asked a robin in the garden to be her friend. She began treating her maid with more respect. Won over by the guilelessness of her maid's little brother, Dickon, and craving his approval, Mary found herself seeking his advice. She even revealed to him the location of her secret garden. Eventually, Mary convinced her crippled cousin, Colin, to grab hold of life with both hands. By the last page of *The Secret Garden*, Mary's transformation is complete. She is happy with herself and surrounded by friends.[100]

To make a friend, you first must make a choice to become a friend.

A man that hath friends must shew himself friendly.

PROVERBS 18:24

THE WORLD
WANTS YOUR
BEST BUT
GOD WANTS
YOUR ALL.

I n *The Great Divorce*, C.S. Lewis tells the story of a ghost who carries a little red lizard on his shoulder. The lizard constantly twitches its tail and whispers to the ghost, who all the while urges him to be quiet. When a bright and shining presence appears and offers to rid the ghost of his troublesome "baggage," the ghost refuses. He realizes that to quiet the beast, it is necessary to kill it.

A series of rationalizations begins. The ghost reasons that perhaps the lizard need not die but instead might be trained, suppressed, put to sleep, or removed "gradually." The shining presence responds that the only recourse is all or nothing.

Finally, the ghost gives permission for the presence to twist the lizard away from him. He breaks the lizard's back as he flings it to the ground and in that moment, the ghost becomes a flesh-and-blood man, and the lizard becomes a beautiful gold and silver stallion, a creature of power and beauty. The man leaps onto the great horse and they ride into the sunrise as one.

Lewis concludes by saying, "What is a lizard compared with a stallion? Lust is a poor, weak, whimpering, whispering thing compared with that richness and energy of desire which will arise when lust has been killed."[101]

When you give God your all, you put yourself in a position to receive His all.

"Thou shalt love the Lord thy God with all thy heart, and with all thy soul, and with all thy mind."

MATTHEW 22:37

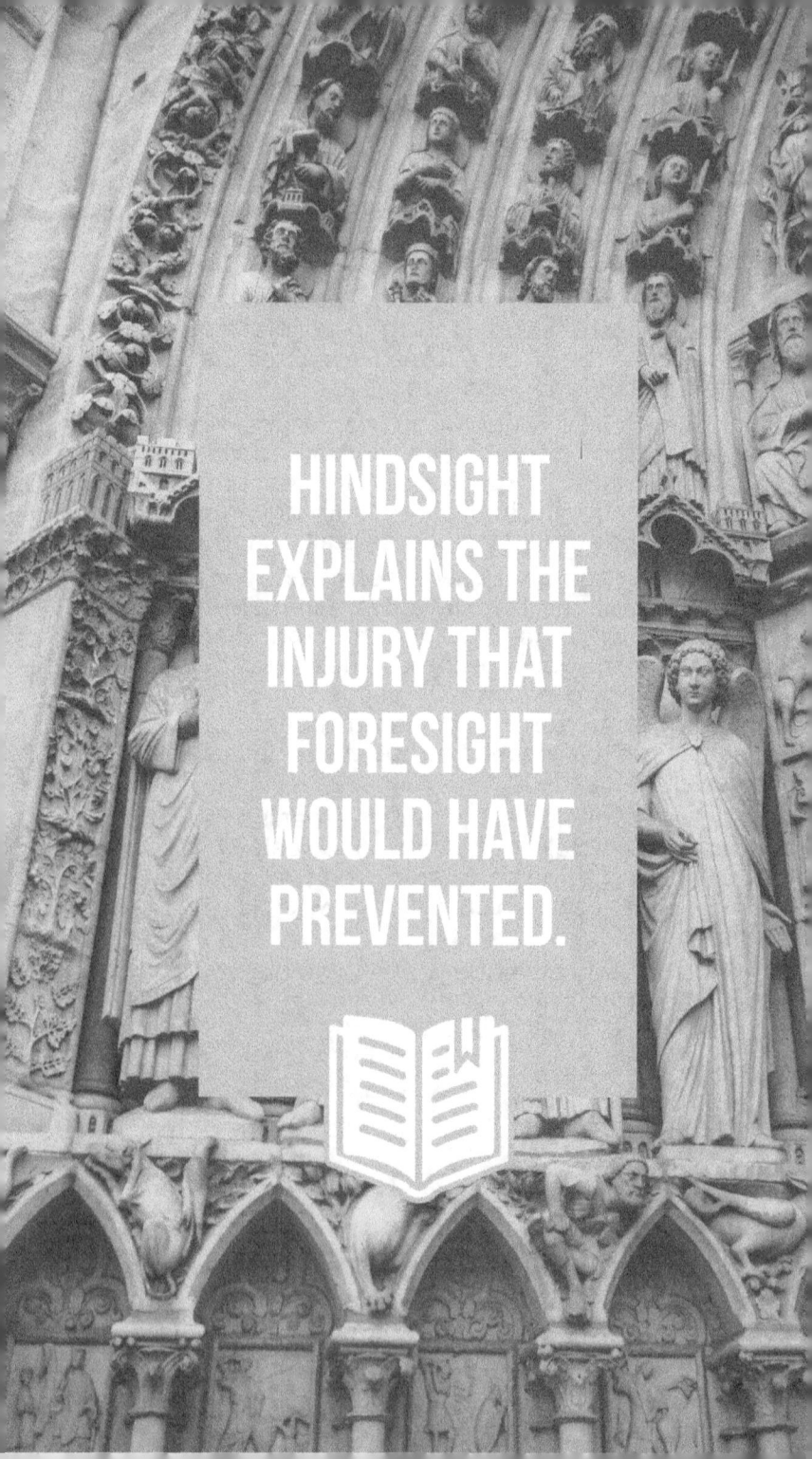

I n 1269, Kublai Khan sent a request from Peking to Rome for "a hundred wise men of the Christian religion . . . And so I shall be baptized, and when I shall be baptized all my barons and great men will be baptized, and their subjects baptized, and so there will be more Christians here than there are in your parts."

At the time Khan wrote, the Mongols were wavering in their choice of religion. Khan had been introduced to Christian concepts and was ready and willing to turn the tide of his people strongly in support of Christianity.

Pope Gregory X answered Khan's request by sending only two Dominican friars. They traveled as far as Armenia, but could endure no longer and returned home.

And so passed the greatest missionary opportunity in the history of the church. The fate of all Asia may very well have been different had Gregory fulfilled Khan's request. The greatest mass religious movement the world has ever seen might have happened, but didn't, all for want of one hundred Christian servants willing to answer a call.[102]

When others ask for your help, be sure to weigh your answer. Eternity may lie in the balance.

Do not forsake wisdom, and she will protect you . . . When you walk, your steps will not be hampered; when you run, you will not stumble.

PROVERBS 4:6,12 NIV

GREATNESS
LIES NOT IN
BEING STRONG,
BUT THE RIGHT
USE OF
STRENGTH.

During World War II, a chief petty officer was killed. His ship had visited a hundred ports. At most ports, he had purchased something for his children—a grass skirt, a model outrigger canoe, a drum, a war club, a bolt of batik cloth, a flowered lei. He had looked forward to bringing the gifts home to his family for Christmas.

After he was killed, his commanding officer sent the presents to his wife in Texas. When his sea bag arrived, however, his widow discovered that all the souvenirs were missing. They had been stolen en route. The publisher of the Fort Worth *Star Telegram* heard of this tragedy and wrote Admiral Chester W. Nimitz about it. *It was almost Christmas. Couldn't something be done?*

At the time, Nimitz was responsible for all naval and military operations over millions of square miles in the Pacific. However, he managed to take a few minutes to issue an order to the admiral in charge of Fleet Recreation. Planes attached to Fleet Recreation were ordered to fly to every port in the Pacific, where officers and men were to scour the island bases in search of replacement souvenirs. The navy plane then winged its way to Texas with a cargo of Christmas love from a war hero.[103]

Doing the right thing doesn't come automatically; it always requires strength of character and the willingness to give.

Be strong in the Lord, and in the power of his might.

EPHESIANS 6:10

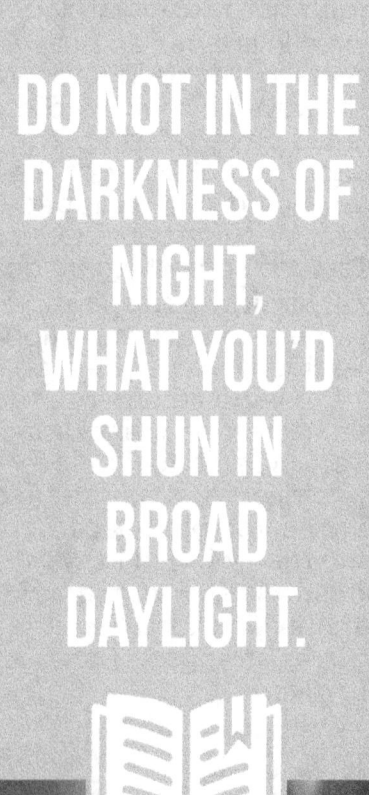

DO NOT IN THE
DARKNESS OF
NIGHT,
WHAT YOU'D
SHUN IN
BROAD
DAYLIGHT.

A man and his girlfriend once went into a fast-food restaurant and ordered a bag of chicken to go. Moments earlier, the manager had placed the day's cash in a bag, and set it at the side of the serving counter. When the clerk reached for the couples order, he mistakenly picked up the bag of money. They paid for their chicken, got in their car, and drove to a park for a picnic. When they opened the bag, they found that there were no drumsticks, only greenbacks!

After briefly discussing their find, the couple decided the right thing to do was to return the money. When they arrived at the restaurant, the manager was ecstatic. "I can't believe it!" he said. "I'm calling the paper. They'll take your picture and run the story for sure. You've got to be the two most honest people in this city."

The young man hurriedly replied, "No, please don't call the paper! You see I'm a married man, but this woman is not my wife."[104]

Many people await the secret cloak of night's darkness before they commit their evil deeds, when in fact, they have already created darkness in their own souls. The light of the Truth will illuminate any situation and expose it for what it is.

> The night is far spent, the day is at hand: let us therefore cast off the works of darkness, and let us put on the armour of light.
>
> ROMANS 13:12

IF SILENCE IS
GOLDEN,
NOT MANY
PEOPLE CAN
BE ARRESTED
FOR
HOARDING.

First, somebody told it,
Then the room couldn't hold it,
So the busy tongues rolled it
Till they got it outside.

Then the crowd came across it,
And never once lost it,
But tossed it and tossed it,
Till it grew long and wide.

This lie brought forth others,
Dark sisters and brothers,
And fathers and mothers—
A terrible crew.

And while headlong they hurried,
The people they flurried,
And troubled and worried,
As lies always do.

And so evil-bodied,
This monster lay goaded,
Till at last it exploded
In smoke and in shame.

Then from mud and from mire
The pieces flew higher,
And hit the sad victim
And killed a good name.[105]

There is never a good end to lies or gossip.

In the multitude of words there wanteth not sin: but he that refraineth his lips is wise.

PROVERBS 10:19

PERSONALITY
HAS THE POWER
TO OPEN DOORS,
BUT
CHARACTER
KEEPS THEM
OPEN.

Mel was a hard worker, always eager to do extra jobs to bring in more money. During the week, he worked as a carpenter. As a side business, he hired out to mow large fields with his tractor.

One day, he agreed to mow a field of wild mustard and weeds for a neighbor, quoting a price of one hundred dollars. Other jobs, however, grabbed Mel's attention and he kept putting off this job. When he finally arrived to mow the field, he informed his neighbor that the price would be two hundred dollars since the weeds had grown larger and would require two passes.

Mel had his neighbor in a sure bind, since a deadline set by the fire department for mowing weedy fields was upon him. When the neighbor questioned the morality of breaking his original agreement, Mel just shrugged his shoulders. He was secretly pleased that he had manipulated the situation to his benefit.

However, Mel and his neighbor lived in an area where few secrets stayed secrets. Many others who had planned on hiring Mel saw Mel's character for what it was. In the short term, Mel made an extra hundred dollars. In the long term, he lost far more: thousands of dollars of referral work and his good reputation.[106]

Make sure that today's win doesn't give rise to tomorrow's loss.

The righteous shall never he removed.

PROVERBS 10:30

AUTHORITY WITHOUT WISDOM IS LIKE A HEAVY AXE WITHOUT AN EDGE, FITTER TO BRUISE THAN POLISH.

rving Bluestein, a seventy-eight-year-old re-tired salesman in California, still remembers the good teachers he had in school.

There was Miss Candy, who said, "An empty wagon makes the most noise." She taught Bluestein that a person who talks a lot often has the least to say.

Mr. Spangler and Mr. Glazer were very fair, but also very strict. Mr. Spangler, a baseball and football coach, never allowed students to con their way to good grades.

Mr. Lester was an English teacher who later went to Hollywood to be an advisor for a movie, then wrote a story that was made into a movie. Bluestein recalls that he had a habit of chewing on pretzels, and had a good sense of humor.

What made each of these teachers truly mem-orable to Bluestein, however, was this: "They got your respect without bullying you."[107]

The respect of others can never be dictated, legislated, demanded, or required. It should never be taken for granted. Respect from others can only be earned—through expressions of love, honesty, fairness, and high moral values.

A ruler who lacks understanding is . . . a great oppressor.

PROVERBS 28:16 AMP

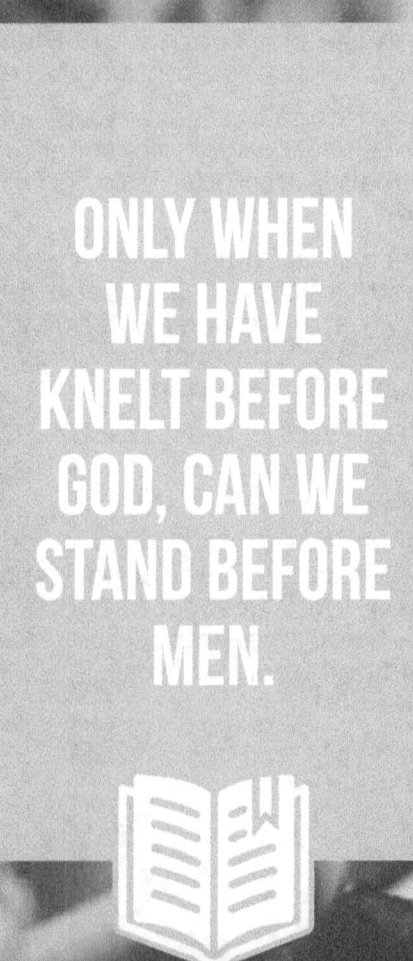

ONLY WHEN WE HAVE KNELT BEFORE GOD, CAN WE STAND BEFORE MEN.

Abraham Lincoln's indebtedness to and regard for the Bible is beyond dispute. He read the Bible in his boyhood and its influence upon him increased over the years. When he addressed the pubic, he quoted from the Bible more than any other book. Lincolns literary style was also influenced by the Bible, especially the writings of the prophets of Israel. The style of his deeply moving second inaugural speech is strongly reminiscent of the Book of Isaiah.

Lincoln not only spoke and wrote in the style of the Bible, but obviously thought in terms of Biblical ideas and convictions, to an extent that has very likely been unparalleled among modern statesmen.

Moreover, Lincoln was a man of prayer, who did so without apology or self-consciousness. He did not hesitate to request the prayers of others, or to acknowledge that he himself prayed often. He regarded prayer as a necessity. He routinely spoke of seeking divine guidance, as though it was an entirely natural and reasonable thing to do.

Lincoln is often heralded as the greatest American president. His spirituality was undoubtedly the greatest reason for the decisions that led to his success.[108]

Never curtail your pursuit of God. It is the most important thing you can do to leave a lasting legacy of accomplishment and purpose.

Humble yourselves therefore under the mighty hand of God, that he may exalt you in due time.

1 PETER 5:6

BY
PERSEVERANCE
THE SNAIL
REACHED
THE ARK.

W. Clement Stone, the insurance mogul, recalls, "Selling newspapers on Chicago's tough South Side wasn't easy, especially with the older kids taking over the busy corners, yelling louder, and threatening me with clenched fists. The memory of those dim days is still with me, for it's the first time I can recall turning a disadvantage into an advantage . . . Hoelle's Restaurant was near the corner where I tried to work . . .

"It was a busy and prosperous place that presented a frightening aspect to a child of six. I was nervous, but I walked in hurriedly and made a lucky sale at the first table. Then diners at the second and third tables bought papers. When I started for the fourth . . . Mr. Hoelle pushed me out the front door. But I had sold three papers. So when Mr. Hoelle wasn't looking, I walked back in and called at the fourth table.

"Apparently, the jovial customer liked my gumption; he paid for the paper and gave me an extra dime before Mr. Hoelle pushed me out once again. But I had already sold four papers and got a 'bonus' dime besides. I walked into the restaurant and started selling again. There was a lot of laughter. The customers were enjoying the show. One whispered loudly, "Let him be," as Mr. Hoelle came toward me. About five minutes later, I had sold all my papers."[109]

Find out what works for you and stick with it!

Let us run with perseverance the race marked out for us.

HEBREWS 12:1 NIV

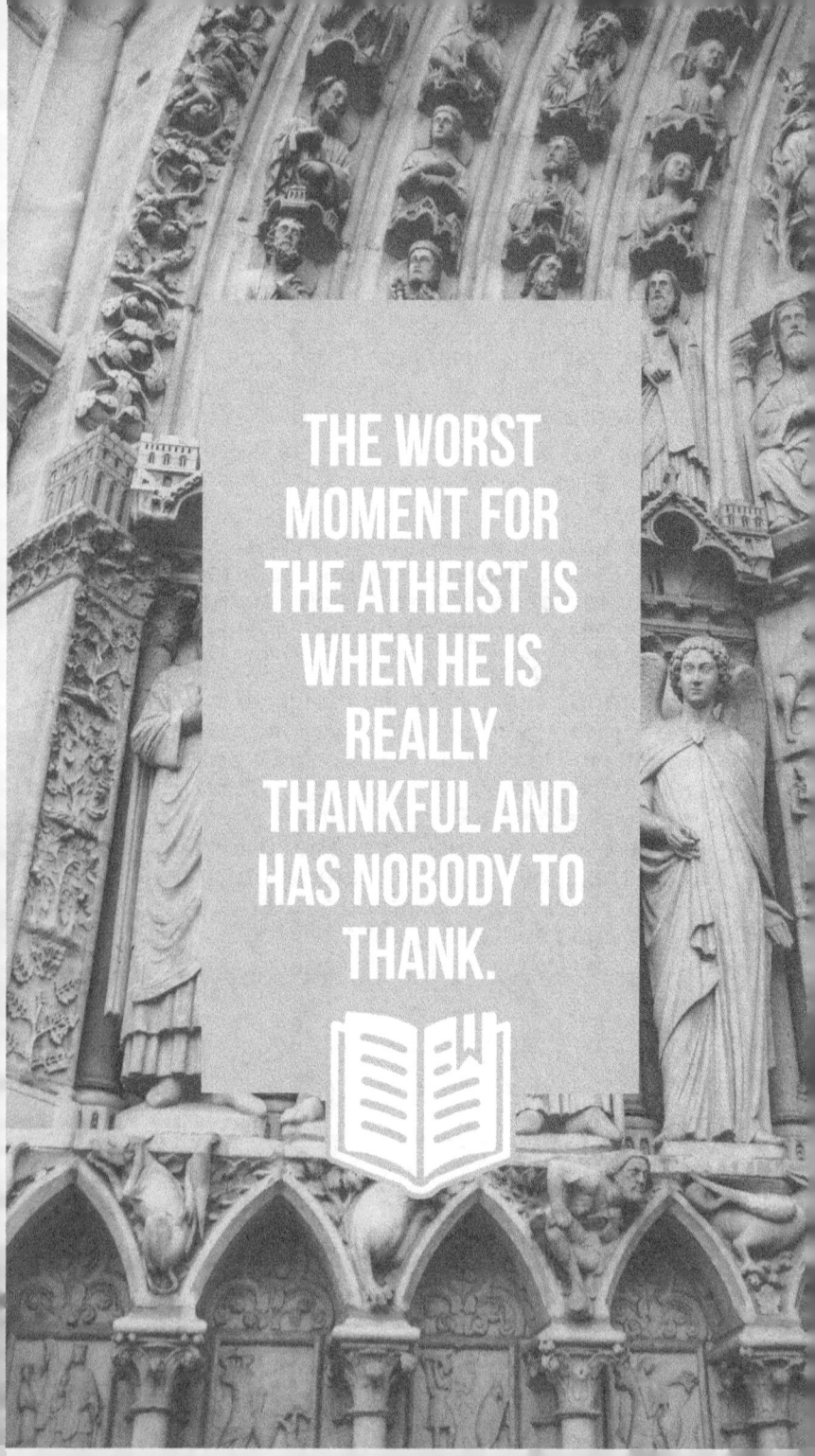

THE WORST
MOMENT FOR
THE ATHEIST IS
WHEN HE IS
REALLY
THANKFUL AND
HAS NOBODY TO
THANK.

Lyman Abbot once paraphrased the Lord's Prayer to reflect the philosophy of those *without* God:

Our brethren who art on earth,
hallowed be our name.
Our kingdom come,
our will be done on earth,
for there is no heaven.
We must get this day our daily bread;
we neither forgive nor are forgiven.
We fear not temptation,
for we deliver ourselves from evil.
For ours is the kingdom and the power,
and there is no glory and no forever.[110]

Most people would agree upon reading this "humanist's prayer"—*how empty, how shallow, how self-serving.* Yet humanism is the philosophy by which millions of Americans live their lives every day. They enjoy a standard of living that is far beyond that experienced by people elsewhere in the world, yet they rarely pause to thank the Source of that abundance, the One who gives them life, breath, and all other blessings.

Isn't it time to pray a different anthem:
"Praise God from whom all blessings flow,
Praise Him all creatures here below.
Praise Him above ye heavenly host.
Praise Father, Son, and Holy Ghost!"

Only a fool would say to himself, "There is no God."

PSALM 53:1 TLB

IT IS POSSIBLE
TO BE TOO BIG
FOR GOD TO USE
YOU BUT NEVER
TOO SMALL FOR
GOD TO USE
YOU.

n 1969, after deciding that he was "tired of preaching to nice people," the Reverend Stan E. George retired from the pulpit. He decided to reach out and share the Gospel with bikers and hippies, the kind of people who never went to church. Over the next eighteen years, he motorcycled over 250,000 miles for the Lord.

During that time, he built a national "Christian Motorcyclist Club" that had 15,000 members. At age eighty-two, he made a cross-country trip, riding his trusty motorcycle from San Clemente, California, to Halifax, Nova Scotia.

As George traveled by motorcycle, he used a number of techniques to draw interest to his message, including magic tricks, jokes, and tales of his odd adventures. He was committed to doing whatever it took so that his listeners would never be bored.[111]

Is there something you believe God is asking you to do today? Don't let your age, your social standing, your present career, your race, or your "limitations" stand in your way. Find a method for accomplishing your goals that you enjoy doing, and which allows you to pursue your "goal for God." Then, rev up your engine and go for it!

A man's pride brings him low, but a man of lowly spirit gains honor.

PROVERBS 29:23 NIV

KINDNESS GIVES BIRTH TO KINDNESS.

C an the aroma of coffee and freshly baked cookies make you behave more kindly? Research conducted at a shopping mall in New York indicates that it just may!

Robert Baron, a professor at Rensselaer Polytechnic Institute in Troy, New York, decided to find out if pleasant scents could increase the "kindness quotient" in a typical mall crowd. Choosing a spot near Cinnabon and Mrs. Fields Cookies, he put his students to work gathering data.

In one test, mall patrons were asked to make change for a dollar. In another, the researchers noted how many shoppers retrieved a ball-point pen that had been dropped. In both tests, people were twice as likely to perform an act of kindness in a pleasant-smelling area as they were in another part of the mall that had no pleasant aromas. Baron concluded: nice smells make for nicer people.

Baron is so confident of his research findings that he's built a machine that should be helpful to anyone who is tired of breathing stale air, listening to annoying noises, or living in tight quarters. It is a combination air filter, white-noise generator, and fragrance producer. He suggests that until the machine is on the market, people would be wise to brew more coffee and bake more cookies.[112]

Perhaps better still, increase the kindness by taking that coffee and batch of cookies to someone in need!

A kind man benefits himself, but a cruel man brings trouble on himself.

PROVERBS 11:17 NIV

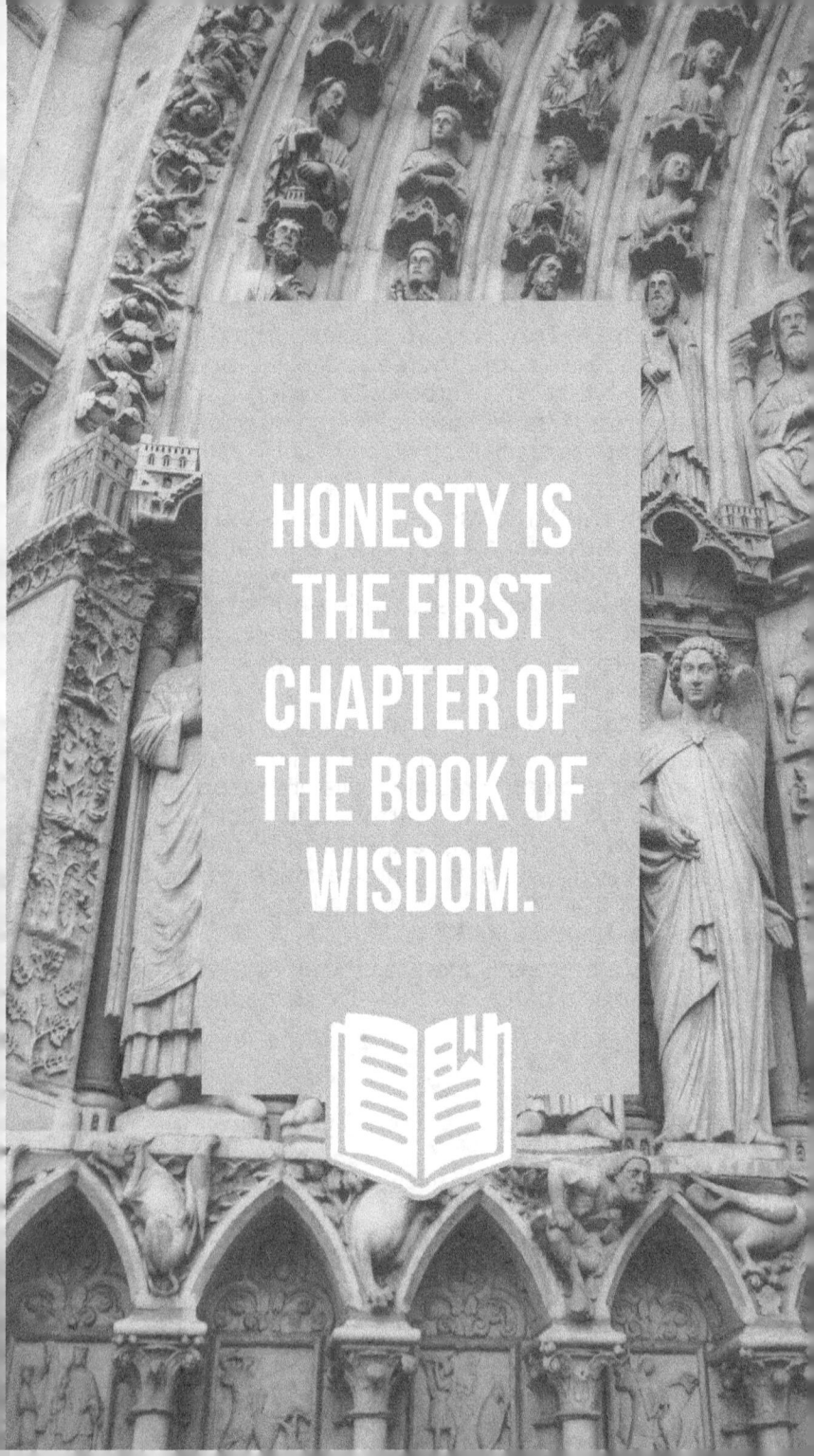

HONESTY IS
THE FIRST
CHAPTER OF
THE BOOK OF
WISDOM.

Bruce Woody, a Dallas County judge, has seen justice served in some unusual ways during his tenure on the bench. One hotly contested case involved a plaintiff who was allegedly injured in an automobile accident. On the day of the trial, the plaintiff entered the courtroom using a crutch, limping and groaning in pain. After jury selection, the judge noted that the plaintiff's attorney was absent. The plaintiff graciously offered to go get his lawyer. Then, he sprang from his chair—without his crutch—and strode out of the courtroom past the jury. Moments later, the plaintiff's attorney walked into the courtroom alone and stated, "Your Honor, we have decided to drop the lawsuit." Judge Woody responded, "I thought you might."[113]

Honesty is not only the display of fair and honest behavior, but a motivation of the heart. A man once went to his attorney and said, "I am going into a business deal with a man I do not trust. I want you to frame an airtight contract that he can't break, which will protect me from any sort of mischief he may have on his mind." His attorney wisely replied, "There is no group of words in the English language that will take the place of plain honesty between men, which will fully protect either of you if you plan to deceive the other."[114]

Remember, if you stay honest in your motivations, you will act accordingly. Therefore, choose to be in association with those who act honestly, for then you will know the motivation of their hearts.

Provide things honest in the sight of all men.

ROMANS 12:17

SOME MINDS
ARE LIKE
FINISHED
CONCRETE—
THOROUGHLY
MIXED AND
PERMANENTLY
SET.

The municipal registrar of births, marriages, and deaths in Hatfield, England, once recorded this name on a death certificate: "Mr. Serious Misconduct of Mill Lane, Welwyn, aged 74." There was no dispute of her entry.

It seems that Mr. Misconduct had actually been christened as Malcolm Mactaggart. In 1939, he had a serious argument with his employer, the London Midland and Scottish Railway Company. The incident arose over his taking two weeks' vacation, when the railway company said that he was entitled to only one week. He was fired for "serious misconduct."

Mactaggart never forgave the railway company for firing him. He decided to adopt the slur against his character as his official name. That way, any time someone questioned his name—which was often—he had an opportunity to recall the injustice he felt had been done to him by his former employer. He used the name on all official documents, including his social security payment book, and when he died, his widow registered his death in that name.[115]

In the end, the long-standing grudge you carry may very well become a lasting stain on your own name. Choose to forgive, and to stay flexible in your judgment of others.

Only by pride cometh contention: but with the well advised is wisdom.

PROVERBS 13:10

IT IS NOT GUIDED MISSILES, BUT GUIDED MORALS THAT IS OUR GREAT NEED TODAY.

A woman was working on her taxes one night when she made an unpleasant discovery: her income from the previous year was higher than she had thought, so she owed a little more to the IRS than she had anticipated. "Why don't you fix the figures?" her daughter asked her.

"I can't do that," she replied. "That would be lying."

The woman spent a sleepless night. She realized that she had been involved in some "little white lies." At the credit union where she worked, her boss had often asked her to change dates, add signatures, and "adjust" figures. She hadn't felt right about it, but had hesitated to speak up. That night she realized she could no longer participate in the deceit.

The next time her boss asked her to "help out," she refused. A few weeks later, the vice-president of the credit union called her to ask if she had altered any documents. She admitted that she had and was told that others in the organization had been put in the same position. She and several other employees met with the board of directors and the truth was revealed. Her boss was fired and a legal battle ensued.[116]

It's not easy to admit you've done wrong. But as this woman will attest, nobody can rob you of integrity. You alone have the power to diminish or destroy it.

The man of integrity walks securely.

PROVERBS 10:9 NIV

THE FIRST
RULE OF
HOLES:
WHEN YOU'RE
IN ONE,
STOP DIGGING.

Bruce Larson writes in *Wind and Fire*, "A few years ago I almost drowned in a storm at sea in the Gulf of Mexico when I found myself swimming far from shore, having tried to reach my drifting boat. I got into that predicament through my own stupidity, something not unusual at all. I can remember saying, 'Well, this is it.' The waves were seven or eight feet high, and the sky was dark with gale force winds and lightning. I was drifting out to sea when the Word of the Lord came to me and saved my life. What I thought He said was, 'I'm here, Larson, and you're not coming home as soon as you think. Can you tread water?' Somehow that had never occurred to me. Had I continued my frantic effort to swim back to shore, I could have exhausted my strength and gone down.

"In all sorts of situations we can make matters worse by our frantic efforts to save ourselves when God is trying to tell us, 'Stand still.' We have gotten ourselves into a hopeless situation and the more we do the worse it gets."[117]

Perhaps it's time for you to take a pause in your ardent pursuit of a solution or answer that you are seeking. Give God time to do His work, and to speak His wisdom to you.

He lifted me out of the slimy pit . . . he set my feet on a rock and gave me a firm place to stand. He put a new song in my mouth, a hymn of praise to our God.

PSALM 40:2,3 NIV

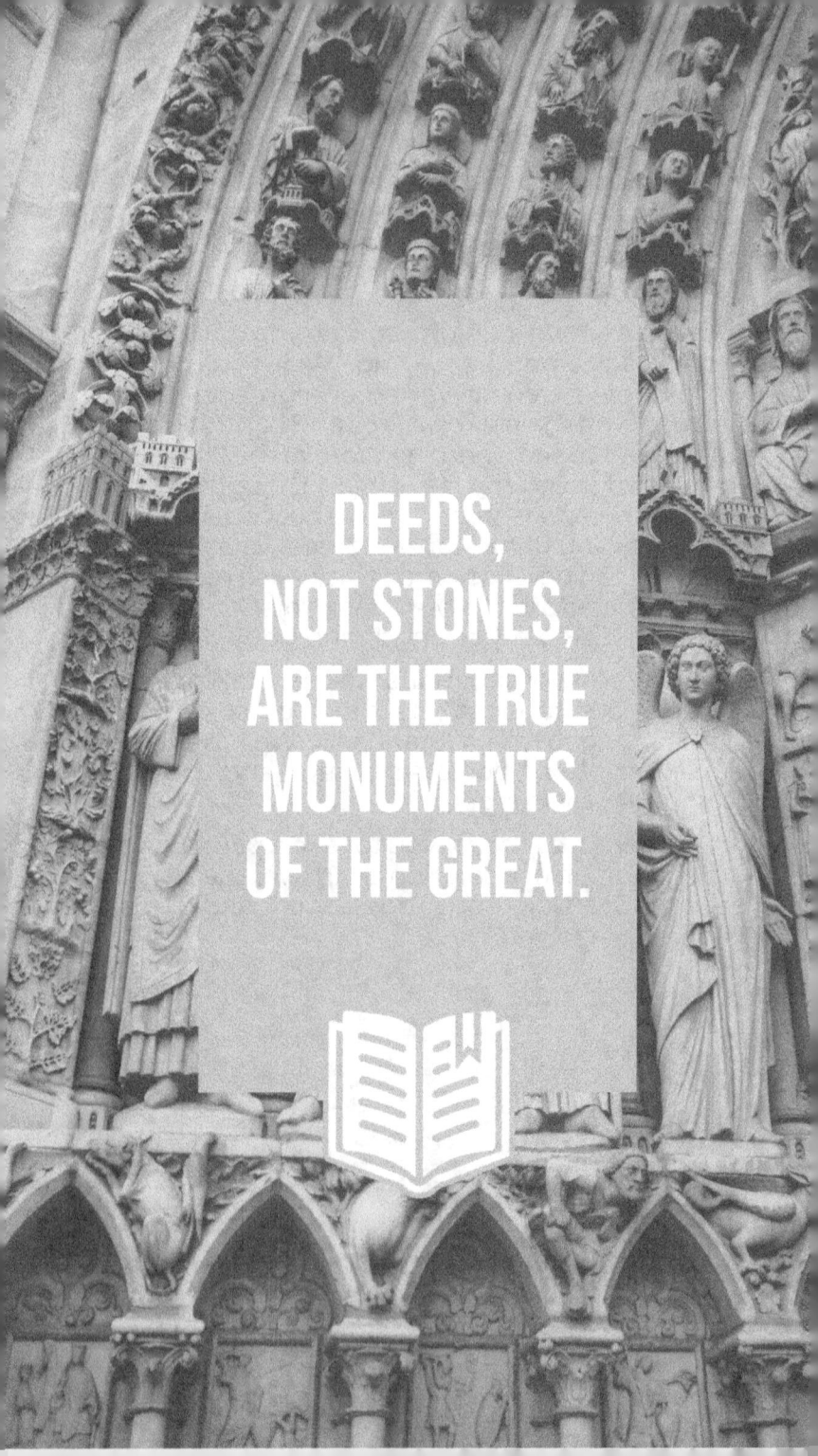

DEEDS,
NOT STONES,
ARE THE TRUE
MONUMENTS
OF THE GREAT.

A private Christian university once had a significant benefactress, a woman who not only gave a significant amount of funds, but also served the university as a member of its board of regents, and prayed diligently for the success of the university's students. She made several major bequests.

After the death of her first husband, she gave funds for a formal garden, which was named in her husband's honor. Then, after the death of her second husband, she gave funds for a student-union building, including a cafeteria, student-association offices, and meeting rooms—the facility bore her second husband's name.

From her own funds, she donated a multi-million-dollar chapel. The university desired to name it in her honor, but she would hear none of it. It is "Christ's Chapel" she said, and so it has remained—no less a monument to her faith even though future generations may never know *her* name.

Daniel Webster once said: "If we work upon marble, it will perish; if we work upon bronze, time will efface it; if we build temples, they will crumble into dust; but if we work upon immortal souls, if we imbue them with just principles of action, with fear of wrong and love of right, we engrave on those tables something which no time can obliterate, and which will brighten through all eternity."[118]

Give what truly will last—a witness of Christ.

"Let your light shine before men, that they may see your good deeds and praise your Father in heaven."

MATTHEW 5:16 NIV

GOD ALWAYS
GIVES HIS
BEST TO THOSE
WHO LEAVE
THE CHOICE TO
HIM.

Phillip Keller writes in *A Shepherd Looks at Psalm 23* that he once owned a ewe who "was the most attractive sheep that ever belonged to me. Her body was beautifully proportioned. She had a strong constitution and an excellent coat of wool. Her head was clean, alert, well-set with bright eyes. She bore sturdy lambs that matured rapidly. But in spite of all these attractive attributes she had one pronounced fault. She was restless—discontented—a fence crawler. So much so that I came to call her 'Mrs. Gad-about.'

"This one ewe produced more problems for me than almost all the rest of the flock combined. No matter what field or pasture the sheep were in, she would search all along the fences or shoreline (we lived by the sea) looking for a loophole she could crawl through and start to feed on the other side. It was not that she lacked pasturage. My fields were my joy and delight. No sheep in the district had better grazing. With 'Mrs. Gad-about' it was an ingrained habit. She was simply never contented with things as they were."

When the ewe began to lead others through the same holes, Keller had to get rid of her.[119]

The Lord truly is the Good Shepherd, be content with where He leads you.

Blessed be the Lord, who daily loadeth us with benefits, even the God of our salvation.

PSALM 68:19

A CHRISTIAN
MUST KEEP
THE FAITH,
BUT NOT TO
HIMSELF.

The story is told of a small dog that was struck by a car. As it lay by the side of the road, a doctor drove by. He noticed that the dog was still alive, so he stopped his car, picked up the dog, and took him home with him. There he discovered that the dog had suffered a few minor cuts and abrasions, but was otherwise all right. He revived the dog, cleaned his wounds, then picked him up to take him to the garage, where he intended to provide a temporary bed for the dog.

As he carried the dog from the house, however, the dog wiggled free from his arms, jumped to the ground, and scampered off. "What an ungrateful dog," the doctor said to himself. He was glad that the dog had recovered so quickly, but was a little miffed that the dog had shown so little appreciation for his expert, gentle care.

He thought no more about the incident until the next evening, when he heard a scratching at his front door. When he opened the door, he found the little dog he had treated. At its side was another hurt dog![120]

Be encouraged, those who receive the Gospel from you are never the same, even though you may not be the one to see the difference it has made in their lives, or the difference they make in the lives of others.

"Go ye into all the world, and preach the gospel to every creature."

MARK 16:15

A LOT OF
PEOPLE
MISTAKE
A SHORT
MEMORY FOR
A CLEAR
CONSCIENCE.

A sobering but highly inspirational event once occurred at a Vanderbilt University commencement ceremony. Chancellor Garland announced from the platform that a certain graduate had sent back his diploma. It had been returned with the confession that in a single examination the student had used help that was forbidden, and though it had never been suspected, and the years had passed, he had never had any peace of mind. He, therefore, returned his diploma, and asked that his name be stricken from the roll of alumni and announcement made of his confession. He preferred public disgrace, rather than bearing any longer the intolerable memory of a single secret sinful act.

The Chancellor said that after much consideration he had decided that the young man's repentance and suffering had been a sufficient atonement for his error, and that he should keep his diploma. The young man would not consent to that, however. "Here is the diploma," Dr. Garland said, holding up a mutilated parchment before the graduating class and guests. "I have cut out the name, and the secret will die with me." The hall sat in stunned silence.[121]

Having a clear conscience doesn't mean never making a mistake. The way to maintain a clear conscience is to quickly seek forgiveness when you have committed a wrong against God or man.

And herein do I exercise myself, to have always a conscience void of offense toward God, and toward men.

ACTS 24:16

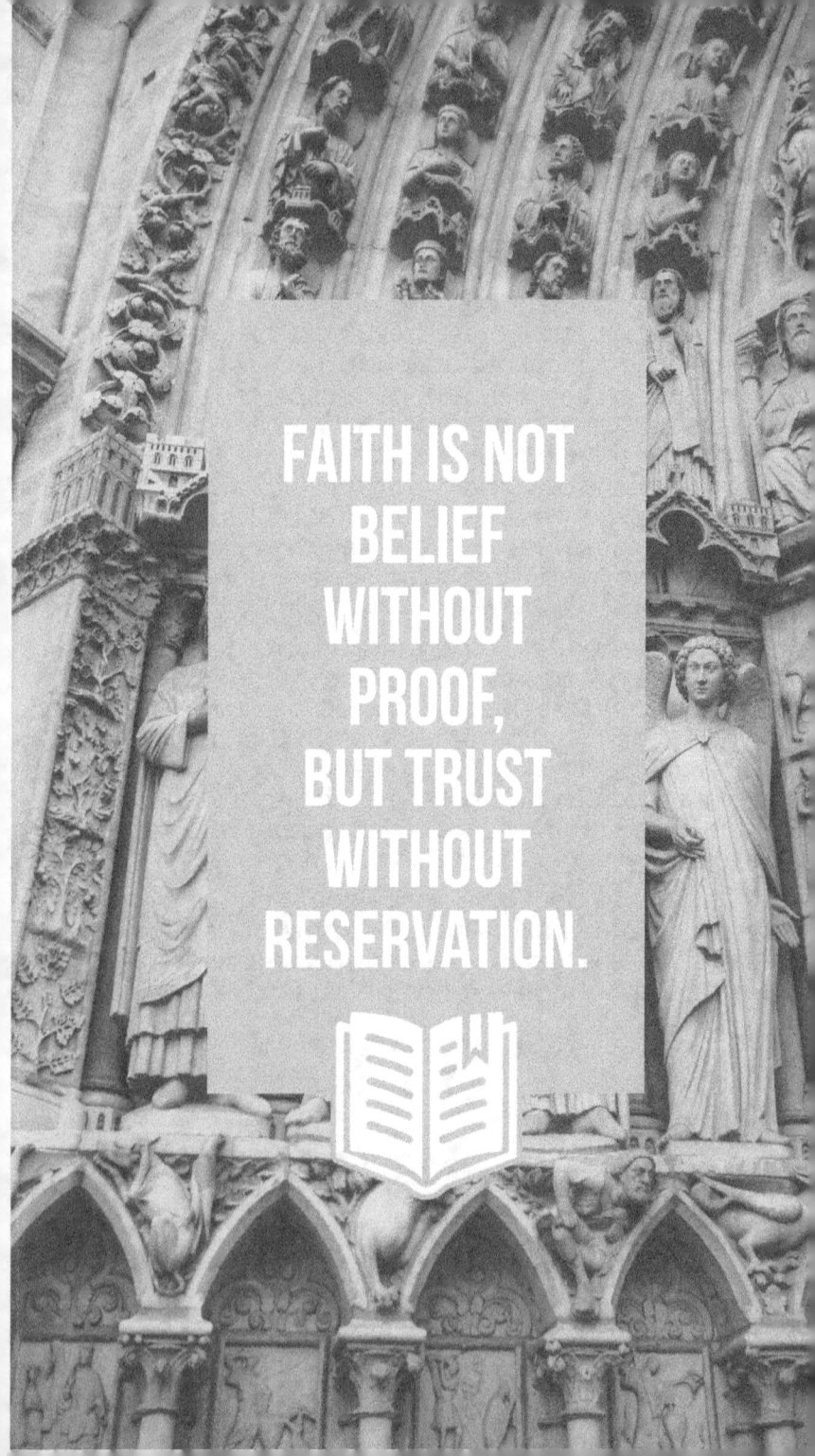

A little girl once crawled up into her father's lap while he was reading the newspaper and told him how much she wanted him to build her a dollhouse. She refused to climb down until her daddy promised to do just that. He made the promise, but, mostly just to get her to move so he could read his paper in peace. She climbed down and skipped off, and the father went back to his reading. The promise completely slipped his mind.

Then one evening, he walked into her room and found her carefully packing all of her dolls and doll furniture into a box.

"What are you doing?" he asked her.

"I'm getting ready to move," she replied.

"And where are you moving?" he asked.

"Why, into the new dollhouse you promised to build me." The father was overwhelmed with guilt because he hadn't given the dollhouse any further thought, much less even started building it. He tried to cover his guilt with a tease. "And are you sure there's going to be a new dollhouse?" he asked, hoping to smooth over the situation with a big grin.

"Oh, yes," she said matter-of-factly. "You promised."[122]

To her, daddy's promise had been as good as a done deal.

I know whom I have believed, and am persuaded that he is able to keep that which I have committed unto him against that day.

2 TIMOTHY 1:12

YOU CAN ALWAYS
TELL A REAL
FRIEND:
WHEN YOU'VE
MADE A FOOL OF
YOURSELF HE
DOESN'T FEEL
YOU'VE DONE A
PERMANENT JOB.

D r. Bettie Youngs writes in *Helping Kids Cope with the Stress, Strains, and Pressures of Life*, about a five-year-old girl named Norma. On the first day of kindergarten, too shy to ask the teacher to use the bathroom and too timid to use it without first getting permission, she wet herself. It wasn't long before all the other students were aware of what had happened. Most laughed, some thinking her predicament funny and others in nervous relief that this had happened to her and not to them. But one brave boy named Norm did not laugh. He got up from his desk, walked over to Norma, and said softly, "I will help you." Norma said later, "We were all sitting and he was standing, so his presence seemed almost majestic. 'And I won't let them make fun of you,' he added."

Norma looked up at Norm and smiled in admiration. She no longer felt alone and afraid. She had found a new friend. Still holding her hand, Norm turned to the rest of the class and kindly asked, "How would you feel if it happened to you?" The children sat motionless. Then Norm added, "Let's not laugh at her anymore, okay?" Norma concluded, "We knew we were in the presence of courage."[123]

Is there someone in your life who could benefit from the reassuring courage of your presence today?

He who covers and forgives an offense seeks love, but he who repeats or harps on a matter separates even close friends.

PROVERBS 17:9 AMP

A DAY
HEMMED IN
PRAYER IS
LESS LIKELY
TO UNRAVEL.

The best time to hem your day is in the early morning, before life's circumstances have the opportunity to add to the fray!

I met God in the morning
When my day was at its best,
And His presence came like sunrise,
Like the Glory in my breast.
All day long the Presence lingered,
All day long He stayed with me,
And we sailed in perfect calmness
O'er a very troubled sea.
Other ships were blown and battered,
Other ships were sore distressed;
But the wind that seemed to drive them
Brought us Peace and Joy and Rest.
Then I thought of other mornings,
With a keen remorse of mind,
When I, too, had loosed the moorings,
With the Saviour left behind.
So I think I know the secret,
Learned from many a troubled way;
You must seek Him in the morning
If you want Him through the day.[124]

R.S.C. IN "HILL TOP VERSES"

Pray about everything; tell God your needs and don't forget to thank him for his answers. If you do this you will experience God's peace . . . His peace will keep your thoughts and your hearts quiet and at rest.

PHILIPPIANS 4:6,7 TLB

SANDWICH
EVERY BIT OF
CRITICISM
BETWEEN
TWO LAYERS
OF PRAISE.

There was once a woman whose husband claimed to be a perfectionist. He wouldn't do a job unless he could do it perfectly. The result was that he had a long list of tasks he never started and those he did start, were rarely finished. His wife felt that part of his problem was a lack of organization.

She decided to do what she could to help him, but was determined to avoid nagging. First, she kept his tools and materials picked up and sorted them for him. Next, she purchased organizational tools for him—such as a small hand-held computer and writing tablets. She worked with him on writing lists of things that needed to be accomplished each day, and allowed him to prioritize the list.

Finally, she encouraged him to do a job as good as he could, but also let him know that a job didn't have to be perfect. She said, "I praised him when he began a job, during the job, and after it was complete. Praise was very important to him and I found he needed to hear me praise him to other people. He needed to know two things, that his projects were appreciated, and that I didn't expect perfection. I found ways to praise him on both accounts."[125]

Praise changes things in part because praise changes our attitude.

Correct, rebuke and encourage—with great patience and careful instruction.

2 TIMOTHY 4:2 NIV

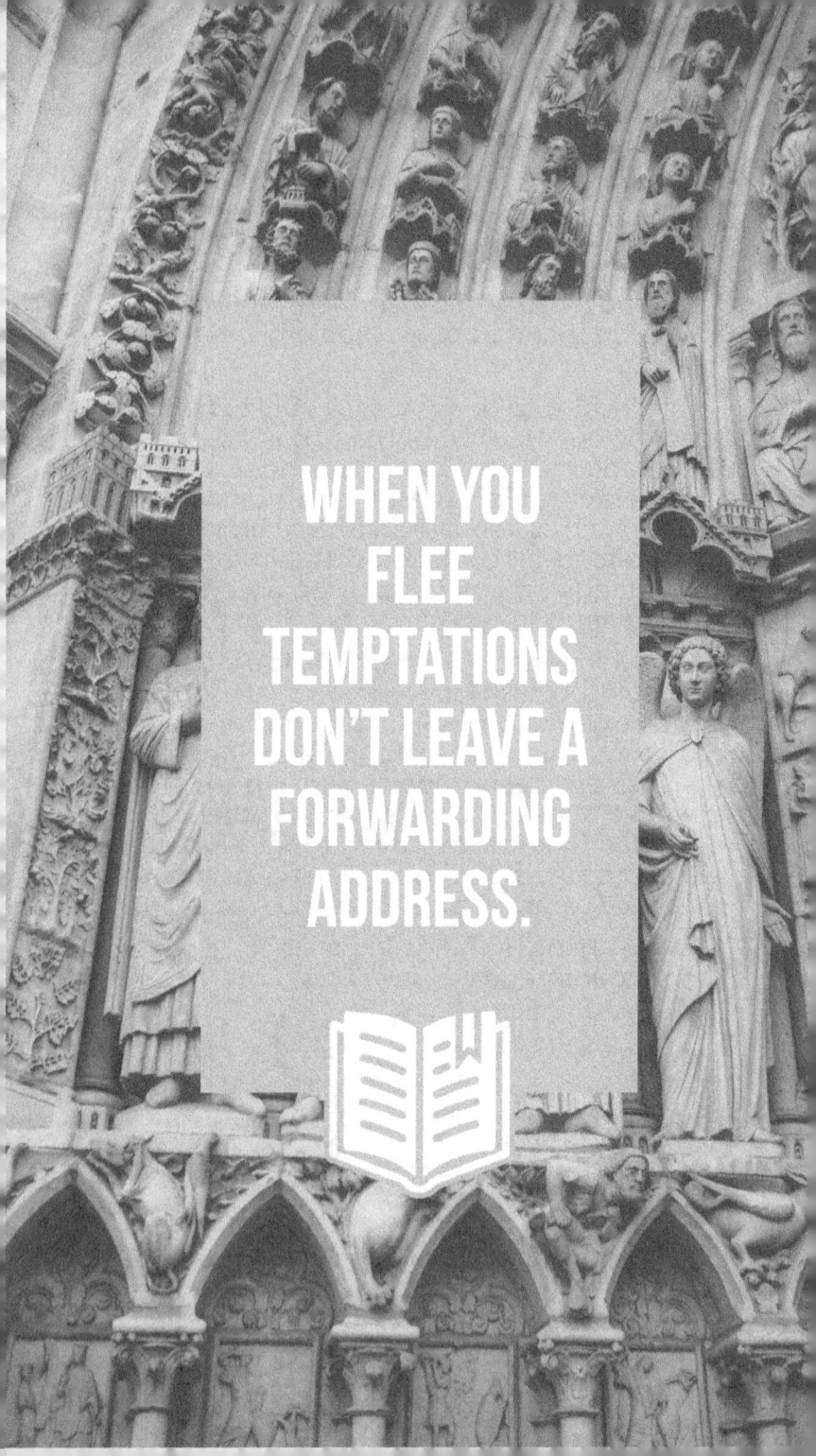

Velazquez Polk and Janet Kuzmaak both grew up in Portland, Oregon, but the two couldn't have been more different. Polk was a tough street kid who joined a gang at age ten, and was eventually arrested for selling drugs.

Kuzmaak was an honor roll student from an upper-class neighborhood. In 1980, Kuzmaak's sister was raped and strangled to death. Authorities never found her killer. She came to regard every criminal as her sister's murderer.

Kuzmaak eventually became a nurse at a major medical center. Polk, released from jail in 1990, was given a job as her surgical aide. She was furious. She didn't believe in rehabilitation for criminals. But she noticed that when Polk's gang-member friends tried to entice him to rejoin their ranks, he refused. He told Kuzmaak he wanted to flee his old life and join a program to become a nurse's aide. She remembered that her sister had once befriended a man on parole, so she lobbied the hospital to pay Polk's tuition while she continued to monitor him.

Today, she and Polk are great friends. She helped him gain entrance into a world that he once did not know existed. He helped sweep away the bitterness that had once poisoned her heart.[126]

Change and growth are always possible—if you first turn away from evil.

Now flee from youthful lusts, and pursue righteousness, faith, love and peace, with those who call on the Lord from a pure heart.

2 TIMOTHY 2:22 NASB

HE WHO PROVIDES
FOR THIS LIFE,
BUT TAKES NO
CARE FOR
ETERNITY,
IS WISE FOR A
MOMENT, BUT A
FOOL FOREVER.

Dean Farrar was a privileged personal friend of Queen Victoria, although he seldom referred to their relationship and never tried to capitalize on it. However, during a service held in Canterbury Cathedral to commemorate the first anniversary of the accession of Edward VII to the throne of England, Farrar told of one experience he had with Queen Victoria.

He recalled an occasion during which the Queen had heard one of her chaplains preach at Windsor. His topic was the second coming of Christ. Afterward, she spoke to Dean about it and said, "Oh, how I wish that the Lord would come during my lifetime."

"Why does your Majesty feel this very earnest desire?" the great preacher asked her.

At that, he recalled, her countenance lit up with deep emotion. She replied, "Because I should so love to lay my crown at His feet."[127]

Anything you accomplish or attain in this life is worthy of only one thing: to be credited to the Lord's goodness and to be surrendered to the Lord for His purposes. As the Lord's Prayer teaches us: "Thine is the kingdom, and the power, and the glory *forever*."

"What is a man profited, if he shall gain the whole world, and lose his own soul? or what shall a man give in exchange for his soul?"

MATTHEW 16:26

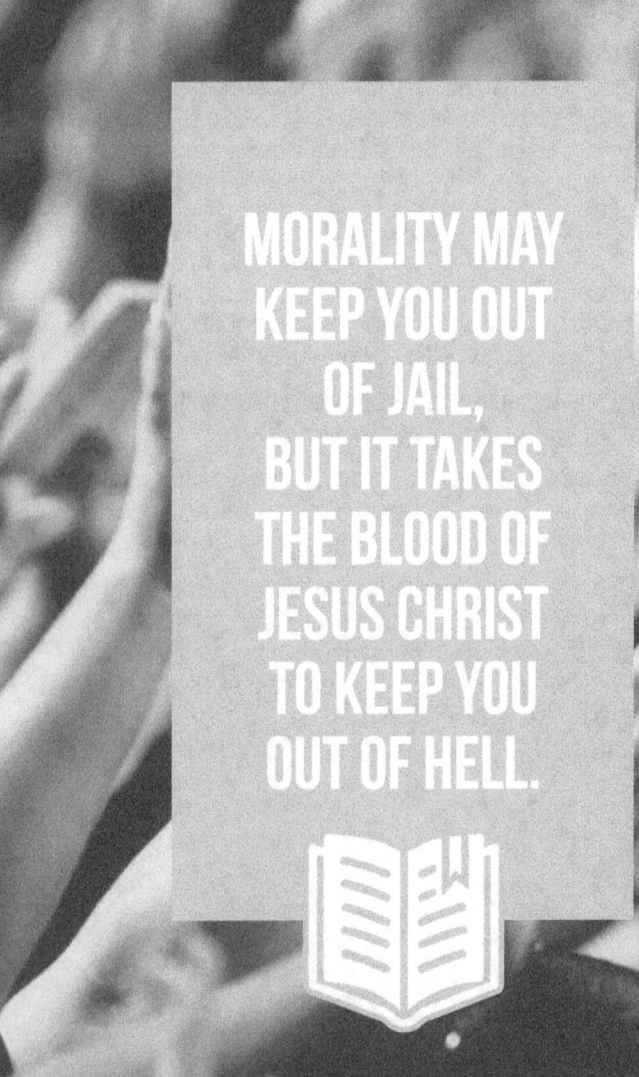

MORALITY MAY KEEP YOU OUT OF JAIL, BUT IT TAKES THE BLOOD OF JESUS CHRIST TO KEEP YOU OUT OF HELL.

Daryl was a hard worker at his warehouse job, but three evenings a week, he took on a higher position. He became a true motivator of men, a highly effective leader. He led a men's Bible study, headed a crew of guys who repaired single mothers' cars, and was a superb evangelist, constantly leading others to Christ.

Then suddenly, he disappeared from the church. Word began to circulate that he had engaged in immoral behavior with one of the women he had befriended. It was a one-time mistake, but Daryl was devastated. He quit all ministry activities, broke off all contact with the woman, and dropped out of sight. For two years he lived in total remorse.

Finally, Daryl had the courage to contact one of the men with whom he had once been associated at the church. He wanted to know how to get back on track. He had repented, felt he was forgiven, and more than anything wanted his life to count for Christ again. He said, "Coming back to church was fine, but God didn't save me to sit. He saved me to serve."[128]

Christ's redemption is *complete*. He doesn't save us just so we can say we have salvation, or simply so we might have clean hearts or live moral lives. He saves us to serve.

In him we have redemption through his blood, the forgiveness of sins.

EPHESIANS 1:7 NIV

COURAGE IS
CONTAGIOUS.
WHEN A BRAVE
MAN TAKES A
STAND,
THE SPINES OF
OTHERS ARE
STIFFENED.

One summer day a father took his three-year-old daughter to a kiddy park to ride the rides. He put her on a small ride which she insisted on trying, even though she claimed it was the "scariest" ride in the park. As she whipped around the corners in her kiddy car, she began whimpering and quickly worked herself into a terrified cry. The father tried to get her attention and finally, he caught her eye. He smiled and shouted, "Hey, this is fun!"

When she saw that he wasn't terrified of the situation, but was smiling, she also began to laugh. She still clung to her car with both hands, but her face—indeed, her entire body—relaxed and she began to enjoy the moment. Suddenly, what had once been terrifying became fun![129]

There are times in life when each of us experiences a "scary ride"—those times when we feel terrified, out of control, and unsure of what the future holds. It is in those moments that we are wise to seek out our Heavenly Father. When we do, we will find that He has the situation firmly in His grasp. He isn't worried about our outcome, in fact, He desires for us to delight in the good work that He is in the process of producing. And in the same way, He calls upon us to help others who are afraid, to impart to them the courage He has given to us.

Stand firm in the faith; be men of courage; be strong.

1 CORINTHIANS 16:13 NIV

On his way back to Italy, Columbus was disheartened and discouraged when he stopped at a convent one day. He asked for a drink of water. The monk who gave him a drink listened to his story. Later, he was the man who spoke to Queen Isabella on Columbus' behalf.

John Calvin, also on his way to Italy, found that the regular road was closed because of a war between Italy and France. Therefore, he had to pass through Geneva. There he met a man who, with fiery eloquence, demanded that he stay at Geneva and lead the work of God there.

While rummaging in a barrel of rubbish someone had left in his store at Salem, Abraham Lincoln came upon a copy of *Blackstone's Commentaries*. Reading that book awakened his desire to participate in government.

George Whitfield was once a bartender in the Bell Inn. Unable to get along with his brother's wife, he gave up his job and decided that perhaps he should return to college. He made his way to Oxford, where he prepared for his future. He is considered perhaps the greatest of all preachers.[130]

A glass of water, a discarded book, a closed road, a disagreeable co-worker. Coincidence? More likely providence.

The same hand is at work in your life.

Who can put into words and tell the mighty deeds of the Lord? Or who can show forth all the praise [that is due Him]?

PSALM 106:2 AMP

AT TIMES,
IT IS BETTER TO
KEEP YOUR MOUTH
SHUT AND LET
PEOPLE WONDER
IF YOU'RE A FOOL
THAN TO OPEN IT
AND REMOVE ALL
DOUBT.

Many years ago as Earl Nightingale was riding in a taxi, his driver commented that a friend of his, also a cab driver, had started to go into a business of his own. "But I talked him out of it," he said, "I told him that 95 percent of all new businesses fail and that he'd lose his shirt." Nightingale asked, "Where did you get the statistic that 95 percent of all new business ventures fail?" The man said, "Why everybody knows that."

"You were wrong," Nightingale countered. "95 percent of new businesses do not fail. And let me ask you this: If your friend had gone into a business of his own and failed, could he have got his cab driving job back?"

He said, "Oh, sure."

"Then he didn't have anything to lose by trying did he?"

"He might have lost some money."

"But what if he had succeeded?" Nightingale said. The cab driver was silent.

"Giving advice to friends doesn't require thinking," Nightingale concluded. "All you have to do is open your mouth, and all the cliches and myths and half-truths just come pouring out. I heard it all as a kid."

The cabbie asked, "Do you have your own business?"

"Yes, I do!"[131]

There's no point in giving advice unless you are sure it is God's advice.

Even a fool, when he holdeth his peace, is counted wise: and he that shutteth his lips is esteemed a man of understanding.

PROVERBS 17:28

PUT NOT YOUR
TRUST IN
MONEY,
BUT PUT YOUR
MONEY IN
TRUST.

A church member was having difficulty with practice of tithing. He believed in the concept, and trusted the Bible to be true, at least in every other area of his life, but he struggled financially. One day he revealed his doubts to his minister, "Pastor, I just don't see how I can give 10 percent of my income to the church when I can't even keep on top of our bills."

The pastor replied, "John if I promise to make up the difference in your bills if you fall short, do you think you could try tithing for just one month?"

After a moment's pause, John replied, "Sure, if you promise to make up any shortage, I guess I could try tithing for one month."

"Now, what do you think of that," mused the pastor. "You say you'd be willing to put your trust in a mere man like myself, who possesses so little materially, but you couldn't trust your Heavenly Father who owns the whole universe!" The following Sunday, John gave his tithe, and continued to do so every Sunday after that.[132]

The coins in your pocket are your best reminder: "In God We Trust."

Trust in your money and down you go!
Trust in God and flourish as a tree!

PROVERBS 11:28 TLB

THE MAN WHO
SINGS HIS
OWN PRAISES
ALWAYS GETS
THE WRONG
PITCH.

Voltaire said that he could and would destroy, within just a few years, what it took Christ eighteen centuries to establish. He hoped to replace what he perceived as faulty philosophy with a better one of his own creation. However, Voltaire's printing press was later used to print Bibles and his log cabin was later owned by a Bible society and filled with Bibles.

We err anytime we seek to earn our own praises. For the Christian, the only one truly to be praised is the Lord God. Christian leaders through the centuries have known this well. Martin Luther once said, "I pray you leave my name alone. Do not call yourselves Lutherans, but Christians."

John Wesley said, "I wish the name Methodist might never be mentioned again, but lost in eternal oblivion." Charles Spurgeon said, "I say of the Baptist name, let it perish, but let Christ's own name last forever. I look forward with pleasure to the day when there will not be a 'Baptist' living."[133]

Rather than exalt yourself today seek to exalt the one whose name will last forever, and before whom every knee will one day bow.

Let another man praise thee, and not thine own mouth; a stranger, and not thine own lips.

PROVERBS 27:2

When Brenda and George's twelve-year-old daughter, Shannon, died inexplicably in December of 1977, an autopsy revealed something they had never known: Shannon had acute diabetes. Brenda and George and their family immersed themselves in seasonal activities to try to get through the initial shock. In the following weeks, friends brought a steady stream of meals and comfort.

Brenda's grief was overwhelming. She had never experienced loss before. She was reared by godly parents, accepted Christ as a child, and married her college sweetheart, a fine Christian man. Shannon's death was devastating. As never before, she and George had to come to the realization that God is totally sufficient and can be wholly trusted.

As she grieved, Brenda began reading books about others who had experienced the loss of a child. Gradually, as God healed her heart, He built into her and her husband a compassion for those who had experienced similar loss. They established a support group in their church called "Lost and Found." As they have ministered through the years, they have been kept from bitterness, and helped countless others.[134]

God doesn't always answer our desires the way we believe He should. But He does promise to be with us always, and to work all things for our good.

And the peace of God, which transcends all understanding, will guard your hearts and your minds in Christ Jesus.

PHILIPPIANS 4:7 NIV

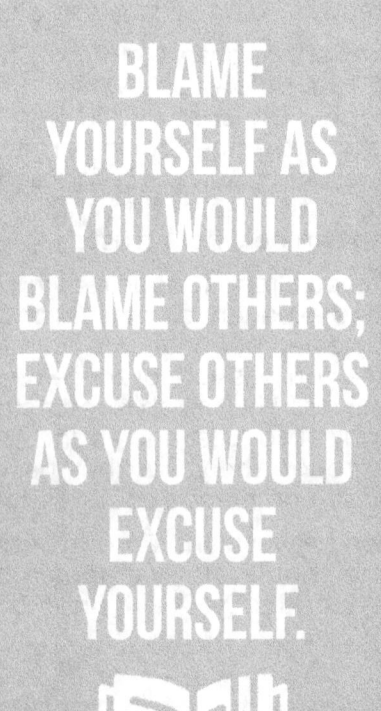

BLAME
YOURSELF AS
YOU WOULD
BLAME OTHERS;
EXCUSE OTHERS
AS YOU WOULD
EXCUSE
YOURSELF.

A young employee secretly misappropriated several hundred dollars of his company's money. When the deed was discovered, the young man was told to report to the office of the senior vice-president. As he went upstairs to the administrative office, he was heavyhearted. He had no doubt, he would lose his job. He also feared the possibility that legal action might be taken against him. It seemed as if within a matter of seconds his whole world had collapsed.

Upon arriving in the office of the senior executive, the young man was questioned about the entire affair. He admitted to what he had done. The executive then surprised him by asking him this question, "If I keep you in your present position, can I trust you in the future?" The young man brightened and said, "Yes, sir! You sure can! I've learned my lesson."

The executive then said, "I'm not going to press charges and you can continue in your present responsibility." The young man expressed his gratitude, but the executive stopped his effusive statements by saying, "I think you ought to know that you are the second man in this company who gave in to temptation and was shown leniency. I was the first. What you have done, I did. The mercy you are receiving, I received. It is only the grace of God that can keep us both."[135]

And so, too, with each of us.

"Therefore, however you want people to treat you, so treat them."

MATTHEW 7:12 NASB

THE PAST
SHOULD BE A
SPRINGBOARD
NOT A
HAMMOCK.

There is a strong tendency on the part of Americans, whether they are in government or business, to achieve as individuals. A high priority is placed upon independence and personal innovation. Every person is expected to forge his or her own career, and to rise as high as possible.

The Japanese have a very different approach. Continuity is emphasized. What matters is the success of the group, be it a corporate team or the entire nation. Each person is seen as building upon the successes of those who have gone before, and then contributing a portion to the future success of others.

Both approaches work! Each has its strengths, and its weaknesses.

The model of the church through history is one that balances both innovation and continuity. The continuity is born out by a fidelity to the faith—one Lord, one baptism, one Spirit. Innovation, however, is accepted in worship styles and in evangelism methods. At no time is the church expected to be stagnant. We are always to be striving for perfection and winning more souls.[136]

Work for a balance in your own life between the old-and-proven and the new-and-potentially-effective.

But this one thing I do, forgetting those things which are behind, and reaching forth unto those things which are before.

PHILIPPIANS 3:13

MOTIVATION IS WHEN YOUR DREAMS PUT ON WORK CLOTHES.

On July 22, 1996, a Japanese junior-high-school student set out in a 30-foot yacht on a solo voyage across the Pacific Ocean. On September 13, the fourteen-year-old sailed under the Golden Gate Bridge, just a few days after his nation's media had all but given him up for dead.

Subaru Takahashi is believed to be the youngest person to make the 4,600-mile journey alone. On August 11, the motor on his yacht quit and his battery died five days later. Amazingly, he made the last 2,790 miles of his trip under "sail" power alone.

Despite his feat, Subaru has said his biggest goals are still ahead of him. "This is not good enough," he told reporters. "My dream is to travel around the world. This is my first step to accomplish this dream."

To prepare for his Pacific trip, Takahashi spent five hundred hours of intensive training with yachting experts between March and July. This was not his first solo voyage. He began canoeing at age five, and crossed the nineteen-mile Sado Strait in the Sea of Japan by canoe when he was only nine years old. Speed was never a factor in his trip. "It's not about beating other people and breaking records," his father has said. "To take up a challenge and grow —to do your best—that's important."[137]

Work added to dreams creates achievement.

Whatever you do, work at it with all your heart, as working for the Lord, not for men.

COLOSSIANS 3:23 NIV

THE TEACHER ASKED THE PUPILS TO TELL THE MEANING OF LOVING-KINDNESS.
A LITTLE BOY JUMPED UP AND SAID, "WELL, IF I WAS HUNGRY AND SOMEONE GAVE ME A PIECE OF BREAD THAT WOULD BE KINDNESS. BUT IF THEY PUT A LITTLE JAM ON IT, THAT WOULD BE LOVING-KINDNESS."

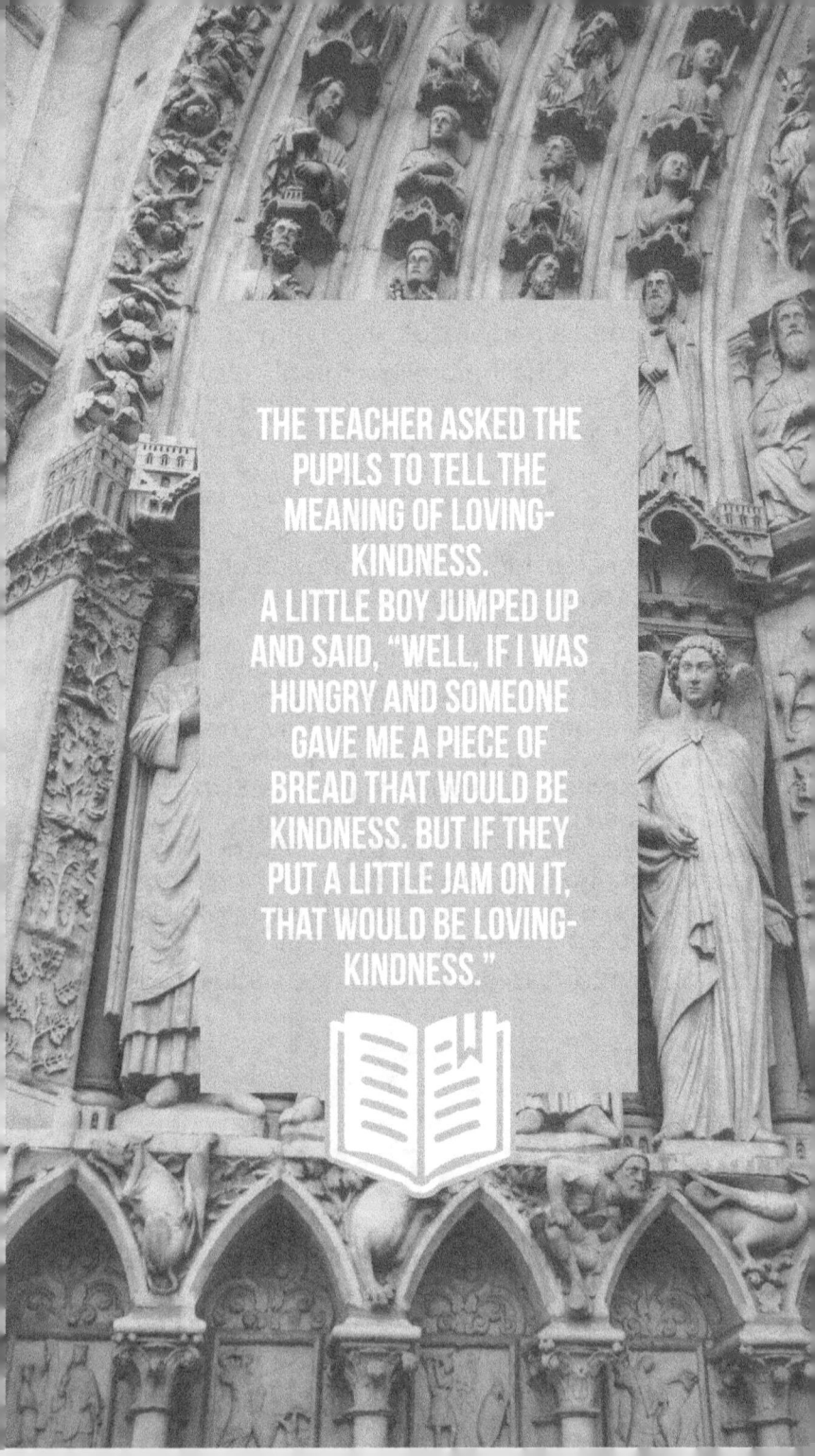

Money can build a charming house, but only love can furnish it with the feeling of home.

Duty can pack an adequate sack lunch, but only love would decide to tuck a little love note inside.

Money can buy a television set, but love controls how much it is watched, and what is watched.

Obligation sends a child to bed on time, but love tucks the covers in just right and passes out kisses and hugs.

Obligation can cook a meal, but love embellishes the table with a potted ivy trailing around slender candles.

Duty writes letters to a child at camp, but love tucks a joke or a picture or a fresh stick of gum inside.

Compulsion keeps a sparkling house, but love and prayer produce a happy family.

Duty is easily offended if it isn't appreciated, but love learns to laugh and to work for the sheer joy of doing, giving, and contributing.

Obligation can pour a glass of milk, but love adds a little chocolate to it.[138]

Love is always the "icing" that transforms the ordinary into the truly delightful. Add a big dose of love to whatever you do today!

Bless the Lord, O my soul . . . who crowneth thee with lovingkindness and tender mercies; who satisfieth thy mouth with good things.

PSALM 103:1,4,5

OUR FAITH SHOULD BE OUR STEERING WHEEL NOT OUR SPARE TIRE.

Faith is not blindly believing in the impossible or hoping for the unknown. Faith is based upon the evidence of God's Word and the belief that what God has said, God will do. Faith is manifest when one acts as if the Bible is true, and then discovers in the doing that it is!

FAITH is
dead to doubts—
dumb to discouragements,
blind to impossibilities,
knows nothing but success.

FAITH
lifts its hand up through
the threatening clouds
and lays hold of Him who has
all power in heaven and on earth.

FAITH
makes the uplook good,
the outlook bright,
the inlook favorable,
and the future glorious.

V. RAYMOND EDMAN[139]

Choose to live in, by, and with faith today!

But the righteous will live by his faith.

HABAKKUK 2:4 NIV

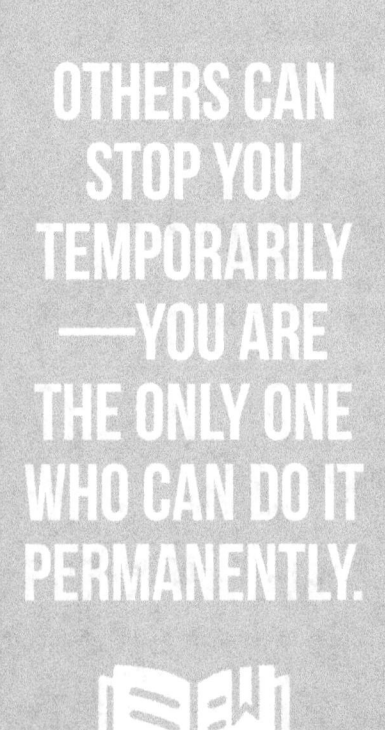

OTHERS CAN
STOP YOU
TEMPORARILY
—YOU ARE
THE ONLY ONE
WHO CAN DO IT
PERMANENTLY.

A man once went to the circus with his young daughter. He was surprised when he saw a group of eight elephants and found that each was tethered by only a small rope attached to a ring on an iron leg shackle. Each of the small ropes was tied to a much larger rope that was staked to the ground. The ropes and stakes were no match for the size and strength of the elephant. Any one of them could have easily walked away to explore the nearby shopping mall. The man couldn't help but wonder why they didn't break free, so he questioned the elephants' trainer.

He discovered that when they are very young, elephants are chained by the leg to immovable stakes. For several weeks, they struggle to free themselves. Little by little, they come to the realization that they can't move about freely when they are tied by the right rear leg. From the moment this conditioning takes hold—after about three to four weeks—the trainer said that you could tie an elephant with a string and he wouldn't move as long as the shackle was on his right rear leg. The elephants at the circus didn't roam about because they *believed* they couldn't. The tethers in their minds were stronger than any chain or rope.[140]

What is it that you believe you can't do?

Do you not know that in a race all the runners run, but only one gets the prize? Run in such a way as to get the prize.

1 CORINTHIANS 9:24 NIV

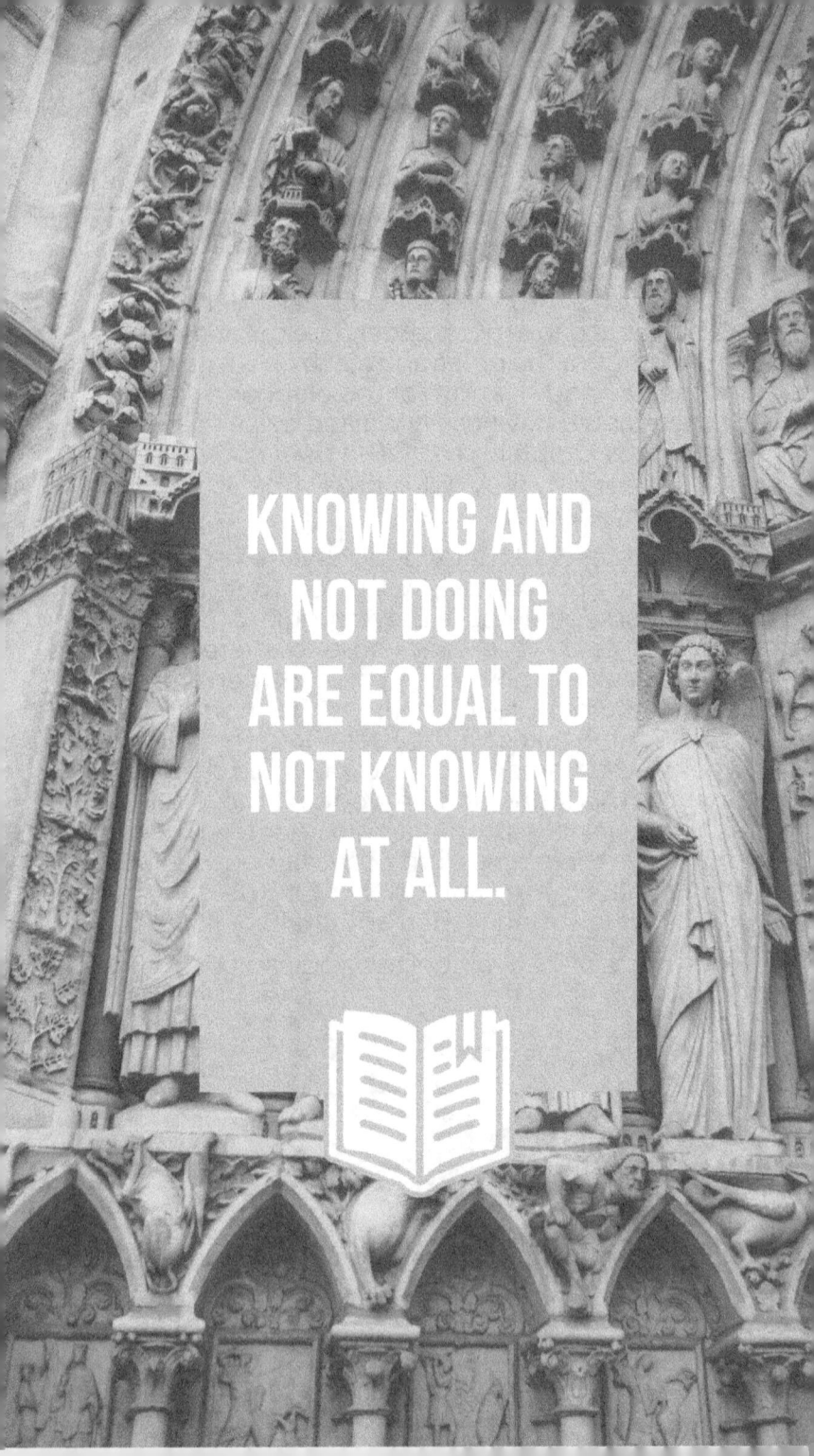

KNOWING AND
NOT DOING
ARE EQUAL TO
NOT KNOWING
AT ALL.

An ethics professor at Princeton Seminary once gave this assignment. He divided a group of fifteen volunteers into three groups of five each. He then instructed the first group to immediately go across the campus to Stewart Hall and to arrive there within fifteen minutes. A few minutes later, he instructed the second group to go to Stewart Hall within forty-five minutes. After they left, he gave the third group three hours to arrive at Stewart Hall.

Unknown to the volunteers, the professor had arranged for three drama students to meet them along the way, acting as people in need. One of the students covered his hands and moaned in pain near Alexander Hall. One lay face down as if unconscious on the steps of Miller Chapel. The third student feigned an epileptic seizure on the steps of Stewart Hall. No one in the first group stopped to help any of those in need; only two in the second group stopped, and all five in the third group stopped.[141]

"I don't have time" is a frequent excuse of those who avoid getting involved in meeting needs. A lack of time, however, is really a mask for a lack of care. We each know the right thing to do. The question is, do we love others enough to do it?

Therefore, to one who knows the right thing to do, and does not do it, to him it is sin.

JAMES 4:17 NASB

CONSIDER THE
TURTLE.
HE MAKES
PROGRESS
ONLY WHEN HE
STICKS HIS
NECK OUT.

One night during the Civil War, a stranger arrived at Henry Ward Beecher's home. Mrs. Beecher answered the knock at the door and found a tall and gangly stranger, muffled to the eyes, asking to see the great preacher privately. He refused to give his name.

Because her husband's life had been threatened recently, Mrs. Beecher declined to receive him into their home and sent him away into the night. She returned upstairs and told her husband about the stranger at the door and what she had done.

Beecher, who never seemed to know fear, descended at once and hurried after the man. He invited him back to his house and brought him inside, where he conversed with him privately for some time.

Later, when Beecher rejoined his wife, he told her what he had done. He also revealed that the muffled stranger had been none other than Abraham Lincoln, the President of the United States. He, too, was in a crisis and feeling threatened by evil. He came requesting prayer.[142]

While we are never asked to openly defy natural law or to show disregard for life, the Lord does ask us to take risks in showing His love and sharing the Gospel with those in need. Love without courage is ineffective, but love with courage can change the world.

"Lord, if it's you," Peter replied, "tell me to come to you on the water." "Come," he [Jesus] said. Then Peter got down out of the boat, walked on the water and came toward Jesus.

MATTHEW 14:28,29 NIV

YOU CAN'T ACT
LIKE A SKUNK
WITHOUT
SOMEONE
GETTING WIND
OF IT.

Stephen Covey, author of *The Seven Habits of Highly Effective People*, once saw integrity in action during a stay at a hotel. He ordered room service and was told exactly when to expect his order to arrive. About fifteen minutes after the expected time, the waiter arrived with the hot chocolate he had ordered and apologized for the delay.

On his way upstairs, the hot chocolate had spilled on the tray and stained the linen, so he had returned to the kitchen to replace it and get a fresh cup of hot chocolate.

Covey wasn't at all upset about the few minutes delay, but the waiter considered his action a broken promise of sorts. He told his boss what had happened and the next morning, his boss called Covey to apologize for the slip up. He offered him a free breakfast buffet as compensation.

Did the waiter have to turn himself in? No. It's unlikely that a guest would turn such a small error into a crisis. But he chose to admit his mistake, apologize for it, and seek to make amends. In the end, the hotel had a very satisfied customer.[143]

If you did something wrong, would you turn yourself in, even if you were fairly sure that no one would ever hear what had happened? The answer to that question lies at the core of your integrity. Skunks always reveal who they are. So do people of good character.

"A good man out of the good treasure of the heart bringeth forth good things; and an evil man out of the evil treasure bringeth forth evil things."

MATTHEW 12:35

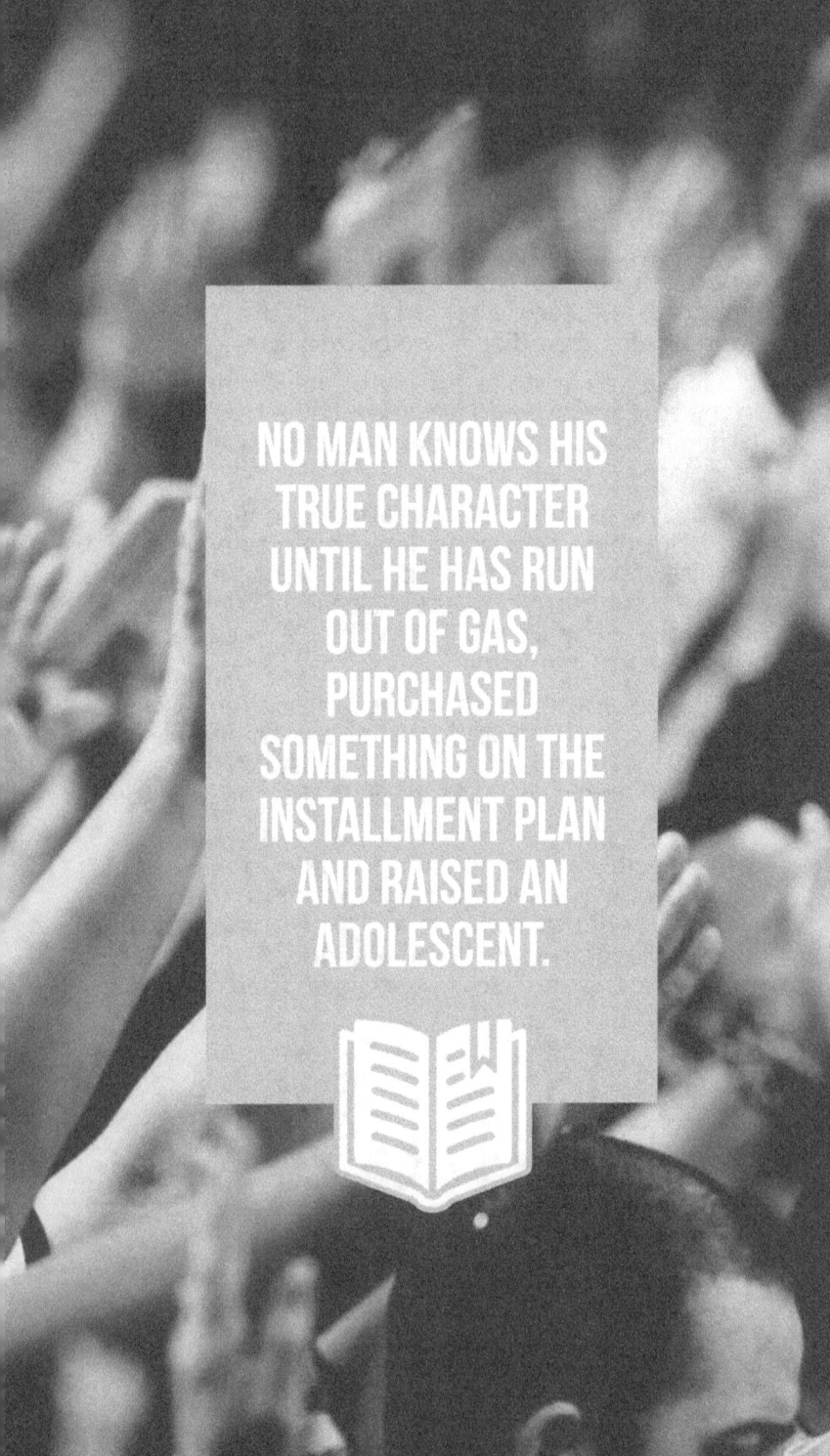

NO MAN KNOWS HIS TRUE CHARACTER UNTIL HE HAS RUN OUT OF GAS, PURCHASED SOMETHING ON THE INSTALLMENT PLAN AND RAISED AN ADOLESCENT.

M ichael Stone had always dreamed of flying. At age fourteen, he began a regimented program in pursuit of that goal. He worked out every other day with weights, and on alternate days, he ran. The program was monitored by Michael's coach and trainer, his father. The type of "flying" Michael chose to pursue was pole vaulting.

Besides being an athlete, Michael was an honor-roll student, and he helped his parents with their farm chores. He was a young man of extreme dedication and discipline.

At age seventeen, Michael faced his greatest athletic challenge. About 20,000 people watched as the pole was set at seventeen feet—three inches higher than Michael's personal best. He cleared it, and then cleared it again at seventeen feet two inches and again at seventeen feet four inches.

In facing his final vault, he was attempting to fly nine inches higher than he ever had. Taking deep breaths to relieve his tension, he sprinted down the runway. His takeoff was effortless, he began to fly. Michael cleared the bar, setting a new National and International Junior Olympics record. His years of practice and perseverance in pursuit of a goal had resulted in victory, one made even more sweet by the fact that Michael Stone is blind.[144]

Choose to endure today in the pursuit of your goals—they are within reach!

Consider it all joy, my brethren, when you encounter various trials, knowing that the testing of your faith produces endurance.

JAMES 1:2,3 NASB

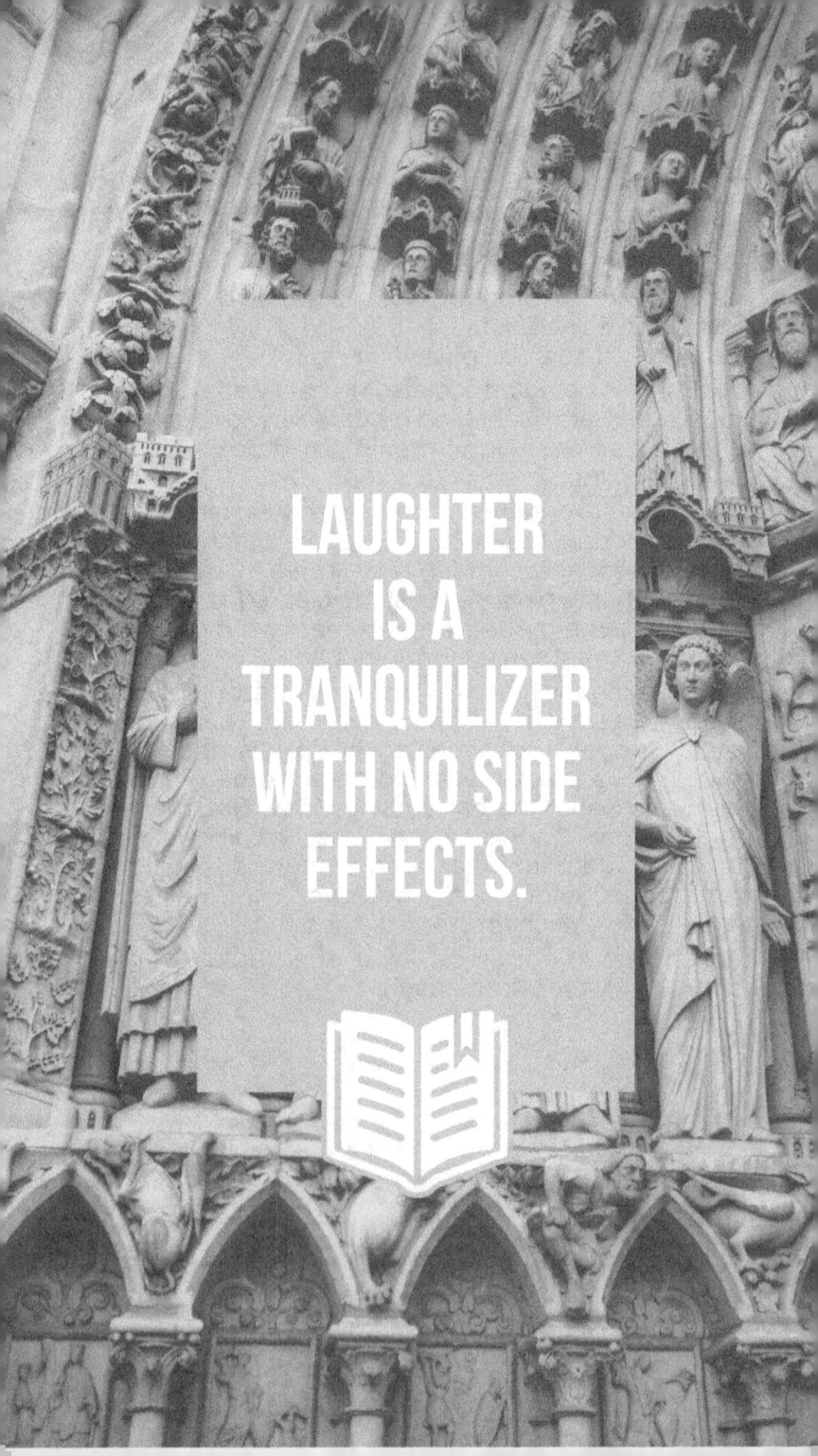

LAUGHTER
IS A
TRANQUILIZER
WITH NO SIDE
EFFECTS.

Jay Kesler once wrote in *Campus Life* magazine, "There are two ways of handling pressure. One is illustrated by a bathysphere, the miniature submarine used to explore the ocean in places so deep that the water pressure would crush a conventional submarine like an aluminum can. Bathyspheres compensate with plate steel several inches thick, which keeps the water out but also makes them heavy and hard to maneuver. Inside they're cramped.

"When these craft descend to the ocean floor, however, they find they're not alone. When their lights are turned on and you look through the tiny, thick plate-glass windows, what do you see? Fish!

"These fish cope with extreme pressure in an entirely different way. They don't build thick skins: they remain supple and free. They compensate for the outside pressure through equal and opposite pressure inside themselves.

"Christians, likewise, don't have to be hard and thick-skinned—as long as they appropriate God's power within to equal the pressure without."[145]

Laughter is one of God's great gifts to us to help us "equalize" the pressures of life. It helps keep us from exploding, or imploding. To release tension and refresh your soul, engage in hearty laughter today!

A merry heart doeth good like a medicine.

PROVERBS 17:22

IT'S NOT YOUR OUTLOOK BUT YOUR "UPLOOK" THAT COUNTS.

A minister once went to the hospital to visit a friend named Ruth. She and her husband had served as missionaries for more than twenty years. It seemed incongruous to the minister that this woman should now be suffering in the final stages of inoperable lung cancer. She had never smoked or done anything else normally associated with lung disease. Rounds of agonizing chemotherapy had taken their toll and now even that treatment had been abandoned. Ruth was left to wait for inevitable death. The minister quickly prayed about what he might say to her, but he soon found that the Lord had led him to her room to listen, not to talk.

Other than her loss of hair, Ruth showed no signs of advanced cancer. She radiated peace as she began to tell the minister how thankful she was that God had allowed her to walk down this path of suffering. "I've always been a Martha," she said, "too busy serving to take the time to sit at the feet of Jesus, but God has used this cancer to slow me down so that I can get to know Him in ways I never did before." The minister left her room encouraged, not downcast. He had been asking God why Ruth had to suffer. Meanwhile, Ruth was thanking Him for the experience!
146

Whatever your question today—God has an answer. Whatever your need—He has a solution.

> Behold, as the eyes of servants look unto the hand of their masters; and as the eyes of a maiden unto the hand of her mistress; so our eyes wait upon the Lord our God.
>
> PSALM 123:2

A WINNER MAKES COMMITMENTS; A LOSER MAKES PROMISES.

Michael Jordan has said about his commitment to playing the game of basketball: "I approached practices the same way I approached games. You can't turn it on and off like a faucet. I couldn't dog it during practice and then, when I needed that extra push late in the game, expect it to be there. But that's how a lot of people approach things. And that's why a lot of people fail. They sound like they're committed to being the best they can be. They say all the right things, make all the proper appearances. But when it comes right down to it, they're looking for reasons instead of answers. "If you're trying to achieve, there will be roadblocks. I've had them; everybody has had them. But obstacles don't have to stop you. If you run into a wall, don't turn around and give up. Figure out how to climb it, go through it, or work around it."[147]

Winners are those who refuse to call it quits. The story is told of a little girl who was playing Tiddly Winks with her father. Her much more experienced father won the game, said "I won," and went on to other activities. Unknown to him, his daughter continued to play. Awhile later she found him and announced, "I won!"

"What do you mean?" he asked.

"I got all my winks into the bowl," she said proudly. Indeed, she had won! She had made a commitment to finishing her game.

Lord, who may dwell in your sanctuary?
He whose walk is blameless . . . who keeps
his oath even when it hurts.

PSALM 15:1,2,4 NIV

IT IS REPORTED THAT MOODY'S FAREWELL WORDS TO HIS SONS AS HE LAY UPON HIS DEATHBED WERE: "IF GOD BE YOUR PARTNER, MAKE YOUR PLANS LARGE."

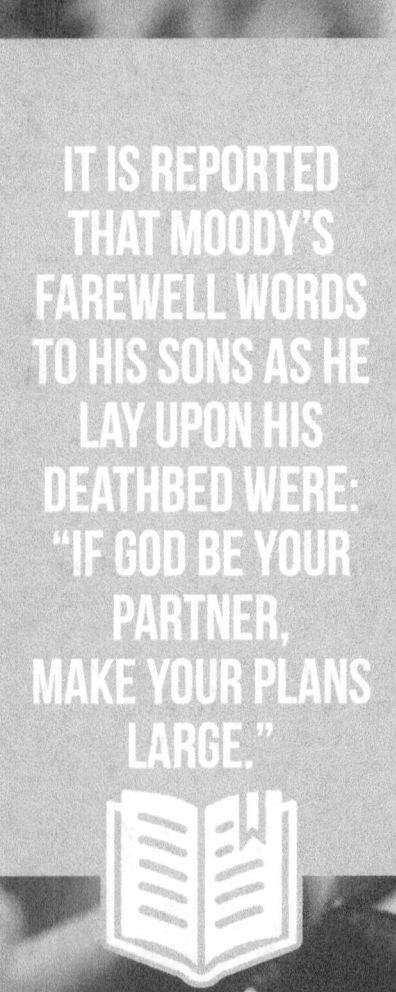

A Methodist missionary to India, Bishop Thoburn, was walking down the street one day when a large eagle feather drifted to the ground near him. He searched the sky for the eagle, but saw nothing. Turning the feather over in his hands, he recalled that pens made out of such feathers had written many historic documents.

He carefully took a sharp knife and sliced it across the heavy end of the feather. It wrote so beautifully that he decided to write a letter to his sister in Boston.

He wrote how the girls and women of India were mistreated and neglected, and that he felt God desired that something be done about it. Then he added, "You are a school teacher. Although you are excellent, there are thousands of others in America who could take your place. Why don't you come over here and start a school for the girls and women who come to my compound to church?"

His sister read the letter to the Women's Missionary Society of the church. Spontaneously, the members responded that if she would go, they would finance the project. Thus, she started India's first Christian school for girls. It grew into a large institution that continues to this day.[148]

Never settle for what is, settle only for what God desires.

I can do all things through Christ which strengtheneth me.

PHILIPPIANS 4:13

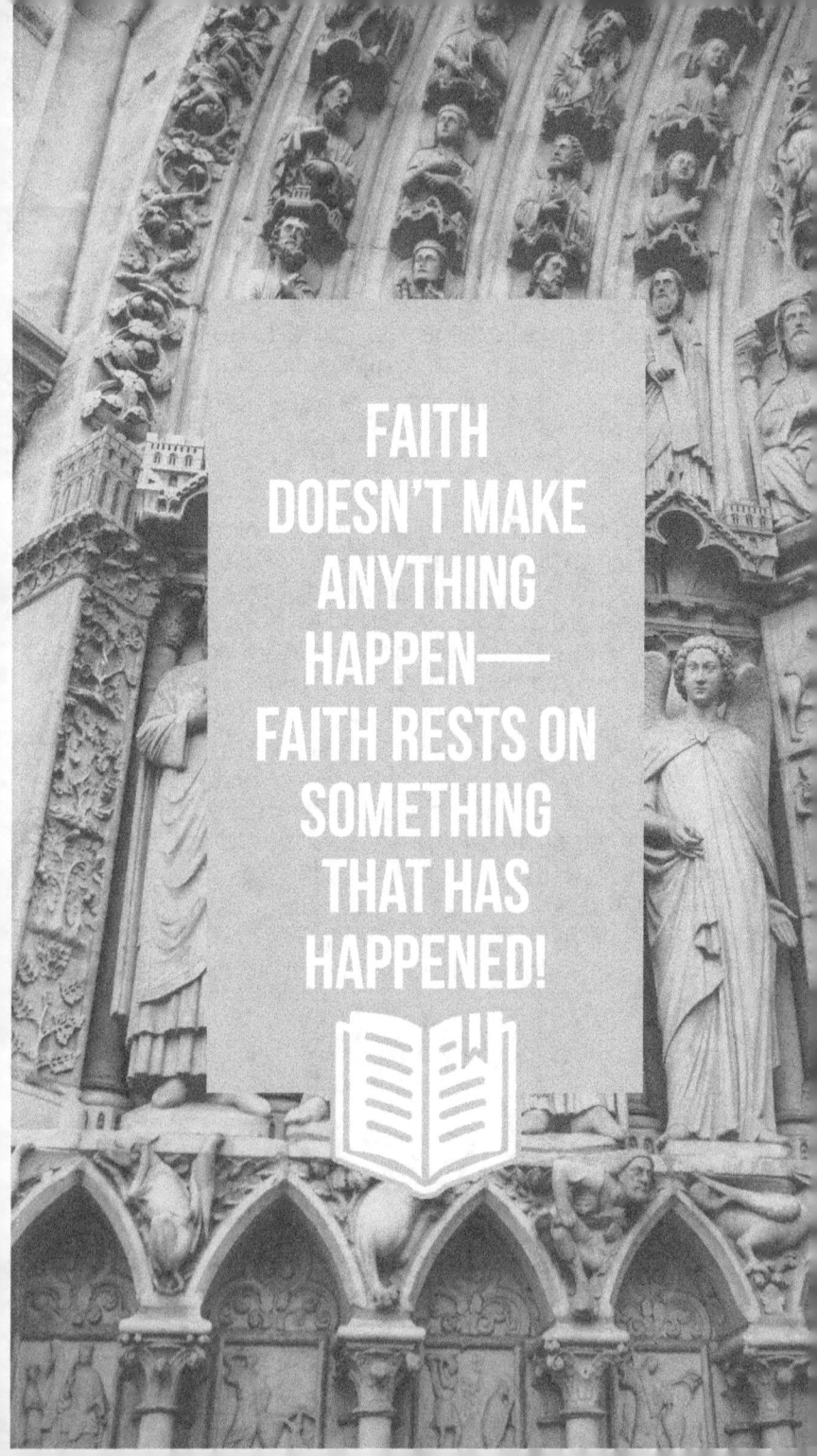

FAITH
DOESN'T MAKE
ANYTHING
HAPPEN—
FAITH RESTS ON
SOMETHING
THAT HAS
HAPPENED!

Stephen is described in the Book of Acts in simple but profound terms: "Full of faith and of the Holy Spirit." He boldly proclaimed the Gospel to all who would listen. Skeptics came to argue against him, but none could defeat him. Finally, in boiling anger the Jews dragged him before the Sanhedrin, the religious court of the Jewish people.

Throughout the accusations brought against him, Stephen remained calm, his face shining like that of an angel. Stephen answered all their charges and confidently showed how the Old Testament—the Hebrew Scriptures—pointed to Jesus and declared Him to be the Messiah. It was more than the religious Jews could stand. They covered their ears, screamed at him, and eventually stoned him to death. (See Acts 6:8-7:60.)

Stephen was only following the example of his master. Shortly after His resurrection, Jesus appeared to two men traveling on the road to Emmaus. When they expressed confusion about what had happened to Jesus on the cross, "beginning at Moses and all the prophets, he expounded to them in all the scriptures the things concerning himself." (Luke 24:27.)[149]

The Lord never expects you to follow Him blindly. He gives you the light of His Word as evidence for faith.

My soul finds rest in God alone; my salvation comes from him.

PSALM 62:1 NIV

GOD NEVER
ASKS ABOUT
OUR ABILITY
OR OUR
INABILITY—
JUST OUR
AVAILABILITY.

A man once saw another man carrying a backpack a well-worn sign, "I will work for food." Although he didn't usually respond to such pleas, this time he did. He invited the man to have lunch with him, and in the course of their conversation, he discovered that the man was not homeless, but on a mission.

He had seen rough times early in his life, and had made some wrong choices and paid the consequences, but fourteen years earlier, while backpacking across the nation, he had given his life to God. Ever since, he had felt God calling him to "work to buy food and Bibles, and I give them out when His Spirit leads." He had read the Bible through fourteen times as he traveled.

His backpack was filled with Bibles, but when the man asked him if he could use one more, he readily accepted the gift. In parting he asked his benefactor, "When you see something that makes you think of me, will you pray for me?" He replied, "You bet."

That evening as the man left his office, the wind blowing strong, he found the missionary's well-worn brown work gloves neatly laid over the handle of his car. They sit on his desk today, reminding him to pray.[150]

The Lord has a unique ministry designed to fit the unique qualities He has built into each one of us. Have you found, and accepted, your mission?

I heard the voice of the Lord, saying, "Whom shall I send, and who will go for us?" Then said I, "Here am I; send me"

ISAIAH 6:8

WHENEVER A
MAN IS READY
TO UNCOVER
HIS SINS,
GOD IS ALWAYS
READY TO
COVER THEM.

Confession of our sins before God begins with a genuine motivation to surrender our all to Him—to admit all that we have done and are, and to yield our heart, mind, and soul completely to His forgiving and unconditional love. We find that when we do, He gives us His all.

Saviour, fill me with Thy Spirit
As I seek and wait and pray,
Bend and break me, blessed Master—
Make me wholly Thine today.

Lord, I bow in full surrender,
Yielding all I have to Thee:
Come and fill me with Thy Spirit—
Sanctify Thyself in me.

I would tarry in Thy presence
Till endued with power and love:
I would know the mighty fullness
Of Thy Spirit from above.

Will He come in all His fullness
As I now obey Thy call?
Yes, oh, yes, for Thou has promised—
If I come confessing all.[151]

OSWALD J. SMITH

He that covereth his sins shall not prosper:
but whoso confesseth and forsaketh them
shall have mercy.

PROVERBS 28:13

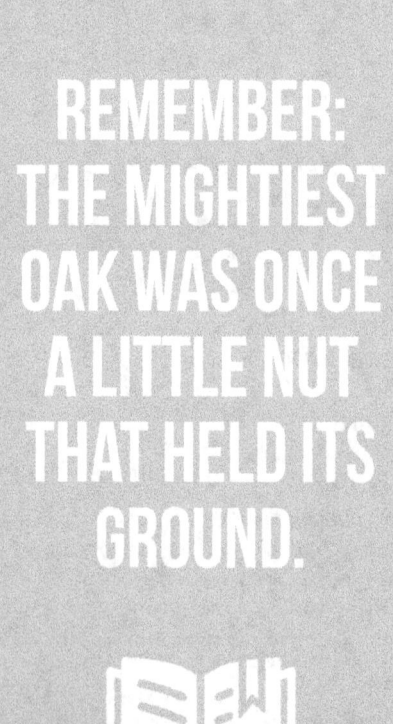

REMEMBER:
THE MIGHTIEST
OAK WAS ONCE
A LITTLE NUT
THAT HELD ITS
GROUND.

George's first job as a landscape contractor was to remove a large oak stump from a farmer's field. It was also his first opportunity to use dynamite—a common practice for the removal of such stumps. With the farmer watching, George tried to hide his nervousness by carefully calculating the size of the stump, and determining the proper amount of dynamite to use and where to place it.

Finally, he and the farmer moved to the detonator, located behind Georges pickup truck. With a silent prayer, George plunged the detonator. The stump gracefully rose into the air and then came crashing down—right on the cab of his truck! George gazed in despair at the damage that had been caused, but the farmer was all admiration: "Son, with a little more practice, those stumps will land in the bed of the truck every time!"[152]

When we face adversity, we often see our problem as something that has come crashing down upon us. We look at the crushed "cab" of our lives and are tempted to give in to despair, discouragement, or depression.

Another perspective might be this: see how close you have come to success, and choose instead to respond to your circumstance with optimism. God is in the process of refining you—step by step—and He has a goal in mind: your perfection in Christ Jesus.

Though your beginning was insignificant,
yet your end will increase greatly.

JOB 8:7 NASB

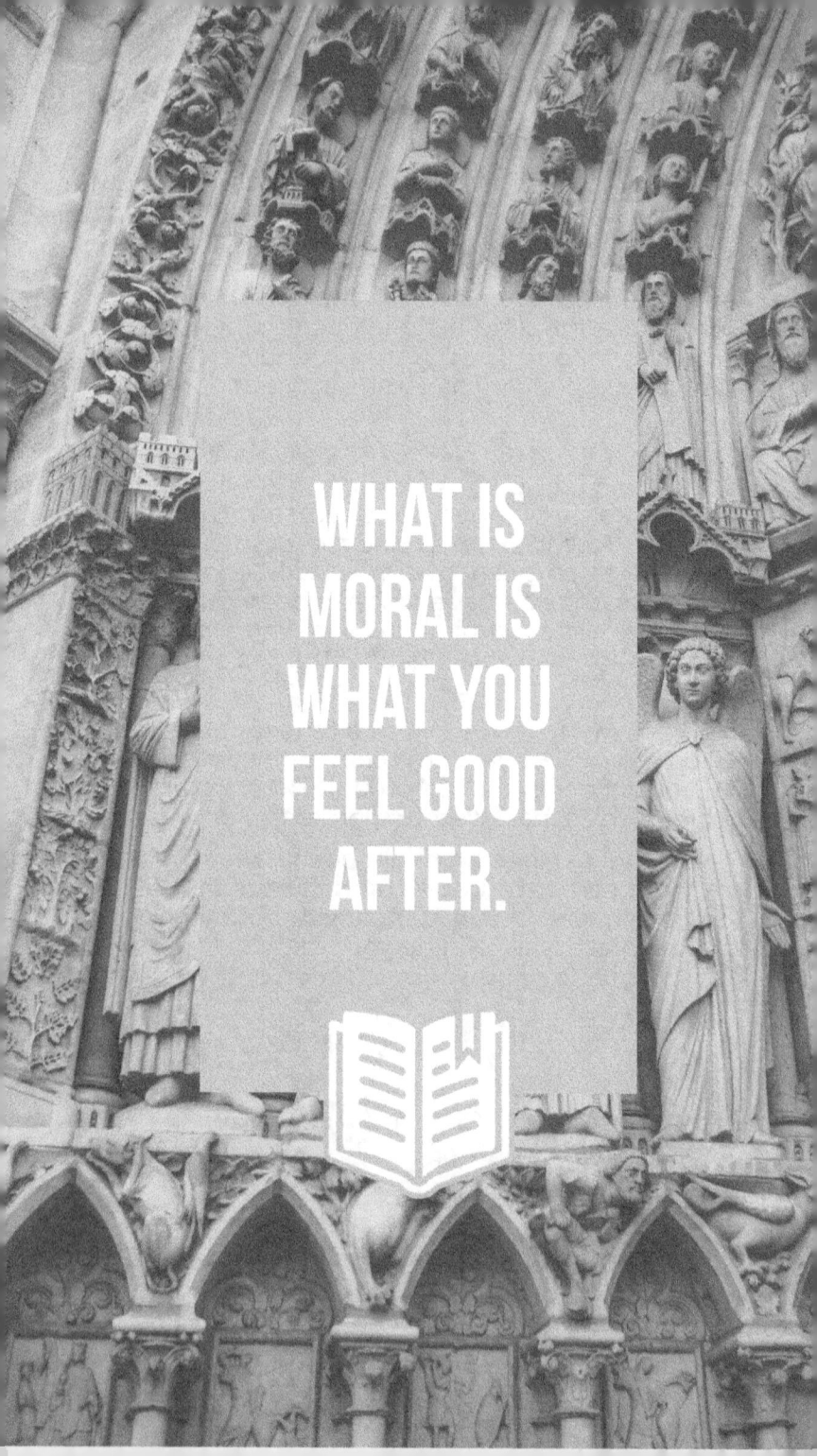

WHAT IS MORAL IS WHAT YOU FEEL GOOD AFTER.

Pulitzer-Prize-winning author Alice Walker once had this to say about the joy of being honest: "When I was a little girl, I accidentally broke a fruit jar. Several brothers and a sister were nearby who could have done it. But my father turned to me and asked, 'Did you break the jar, Alice?'

"Looking into his large brown eyes, I knew he wanted me to tell the truth. I also knew he might punish me if I did. But truth inside of me wanted badly to be expressed. 'I broke the jar,' I said.

"The love in his eyes rewarded and embraced me. Suddenly I felt an inner peace that I still recall with gratitude to this day."[153]

A person always feels good after telling the truth, doing the noble thing, showing kindness, meeting a need, or expressing love to a spouse. We must recognize, however, that the perception of "good" lies within. We must never allow it to be determined by the response of another person—we are to do what is right *because* it is right, not because it is effective in bringing a reward.

"Blessed are the pure in heart: for they shall see God."

MATTHEW 5:8

IF YOU'RE HEADING IN THE WRONG DIRECTION, GOD ALLOWS U-TURNS.

The story is told of a man by the name of Mr. Kline, who felt discouraged and defeated. He was convinced that life just wasn't worth living because no one cared about him. Then, he walked by a church one Sunday evening as service was in progress. He could hear the congregation singing through the slightly-opened windows.

Their song was an old gospel hymn: "Saved by grace alone, this is all my plea. Jesus died for all mankind, and Jesus died for me." Mr. Kline's hearing, however, was not very good, so when the congregation came to the line, "Jesus died for all mankind," he thought they sang, "Jesus died for of man Kline."

"Why, that's me!" he said. Stopping in his tracks, he turned and entered the church. That night he listened intently as the minister presented the good news that Jesus Christ came into the world to save sinners. Mr. Kline responded to his message and experienced salvation. The unconditional love of God flooded his being, as did the love of the others attending the service. His need for someone to care was fully met![154]

To repent means to "turn around"—to move toward God and away from evil. The Lord not only calls His people to repentance, but enables them to repent and start anew.

Have you taken Him up on His free gift of forgiveness?

"If you repent, I will restore you that you may serve me."

JEREMIAH 15:19 NIV

ACKNOWLEDGMENTS

We acknowledge and thank the following people for the quotes used in this book:

Oliver Wendell Holmes

Booker T. Washington

Ken S. Keyes, Jr.

Arnold H. Glasow

Mort Walker

Ralph Waldo Emerson

Doug Larson

Peter Drucker, Richard Exley

J. Hudson Taylor

Morris Bender

Bernard Baruch

Norman Vincent Peale

Alistar Cooke

Larry Eisenberg

O.A. Battista

Charles Dickens

Charles Farr

Mark Twain

Elmer G. Letterman

C. Everett Koop

James Russell Lowell

Will Rogers

Robert Orben

John Buchan

Lord Tweedsmuir

Bern Williams

John Newton

Mark Steele

Hannah Moore

Winston Churchill

Michael LeBoeuf

John Locke,

Alphonse Karr

Amos J. Farver

Olin Miller

Joseph P Dooley

Andrew Carnegie

Dwight D. Eisenhower

Henry Ford

Thomas Chandler Haliburton

Leo Buscaglia

Margaret Thatcher

June Henderson

Dr. Jon Olson

Albert J. Nimeth

Jeremy Taylor

Josh Billings

Publilius Syrus

Grace Williams

Cardinal Francis J. Spellman

PT. Bamum

Mother Teresa

Rev. Larry Lorenzoni

Winston Churchill

Thomas Paine

James Howell

Henry Ward Beecher

Charles Spurgeon

E.C. McKenzie

Anne Bradstreet

Dante Gabriel Rossetti

Thomas Jefferson

George W. Ford

Molly Ivins

Jim Elliot

Jim Patrick

Elton Trueblood

Lawrence J. Peter

Mary Kay Ash

Tillotson

Billy Graham

James S. Sinclair

Ivern Ball

Parkes Robinson

C.L. Wheeler

Zig Ziglar

Lorene Workman

Mercelene Cox

John Mason

Fanuel Tjingaete

Dwight L. Moody

Malcolm Smith

Ernest Hemingway.

ENDNOTES

[1]*The Seven Habits of Highly Successful People*, Stephen R. Covey (NY: Simon & Schuster, 1994), pp. 68-69.

[2]*Illustrations Unlimited*, James S. Hewett (Wheaton, IL: Tyndale, 1988), pp. 247-248.

[3]*Encyclopedia of 7700 Illustrations*, Paul Lee Tan (Rockville, MD: Assurance Publishers, 1979), p. 2043.

[4]*Straight A's Never Made Anybody Rich*, Wess Roberts (NY: HarperCollins Publishers, 1991), pp. 111-112.

[5]*Life's Bottom Line*, Richard Exley (Tulsa, OK: Honor Books, 1990), pp. 246-247.

[6]*Encyclopedia of 7700 Illustrations*, Paul Lee Tan (Rockville, MD: Assurance Publishers, 1979), p. 678.

[7]*How To Change Your Spouse*, H. Norman Wright and Gary J. Oliver (Ann Arbor, MI: Servant Publications, 1994), pp. 34-35.

[8]Jack Canfield and Mark Victor Hansen, *A 3rd Serving of Chicken Soup for the Soul*, (Deerfield Beach, FL: Health Communications, 1996), pp. 322-325.

[9]Anecdote from Paul Lee Tan, *Encyclopedia of 7700 Illustrations*, Rockville, MD: Assurance Publishers, 1979, pp. 132.

[10]*The 10 Natural Laws of Successful Time and Life Management,* Hyrum W. Smith (NY: Warner Books, 1994), pp. 197-198.

[11]Anecdote from James S. Hewett, *Illustrations Unlimited*, Wheaton, IL: Tyndale, 1988, p. 486.

[12]*Encyclopedia of 7700 Illustrations*, Paul Lee Tan (Rockville, MD: Assurance Publishers, 1979), pp. 2058-2059.

[13]*Sin, Sex, and Self-Control*, Norman Vincent Peale (NY: Doubleday and Co., 1965), p. 200.

[14]*Illustrations Unlimited*, James S. Hewett (Wheaton, IL: Tyndale, 1988), p. 460.

[15]*Encyclopedia of 7700 Illustrations*, Paul Lee Tan (Rockville, MD: Assurance Publishers, 1979), p. 1295.

[16]*Against the Night*, Charles Colson with Ellen Santilli Vaughn (Ann Arbor, MI: Servant Publications, 1989), pp. 144-145.

[17]*Lessons From Mom*, Joan Aho Ryan (Deerfield Beach, FL: Health Communications, 1996), p. 62.

[18]*Encyclopedia of 7700 Illustrations*, Paul Lee Tan (Rockville, MD: Assurance Publishers, 1979), p. 2069.

[19]*Fruits of the Spirit*, Ron Hembree (Grand Rapids, MI: Baker Book House, 1969), p. 55.

[20]*Illustrations Unlimited*, James S. Hewett (Wheaton, IL: Tyndale, 1988), p. 182.

[21]*Encyclopedia of 7700 Illustrations*, Paul Lee Tan (Rockville, MD: Assurance Publishers, 1979), p. 2050.

[22]*From Bad Beginnings to Happy Endings*, Ed Young (Nashville, TN: Thomas Nelson Publishers, 1994, p. 29.

[23]*Mentors, Masters, and Mrs. MacGregor*, Jane Bluestein (Deerfield Beach, FL: Health Communications, 1995), p. 14-15.

[24]*Knight's Master Book of 4,000 Illustrations*, Walter B. Knight (Grand Rapids, MI: Wm. B. Eerdmans Publishing Co., 1956, 1994,) p. 179.

[25]*The Holy Spirit—Knowing Our Comforter,* Max Anders (Nashville, TN: Thomas Nelson Publishers, 1995), pp. 159-

160.

[26]*Values From the Heartland*, Bettie Youngs (Deerfield Beach, FL: Health Communications, 1995), pp. 109-112.

[27]*Encyclopedia of 7700 Illustrations*, Paul Lee Tan (Rockville, MD: Assurance Publishers, 1979), p. 1500.

[28]*Little House in the Ozarks*, Laura Ingalls Wilder, Stephen W. Hines (ed.) (Nashville, IN: Thomas Nelson Publishers, 1991), p. 68.

[29]*Mentors, Masters, and Mrs. MacGregor*, Jane Bluestein (Deerfield Beach, FL: Health Communications, 1995), pp. 32-33.

[30]*Encyclopedia of 7700 Illustrations*, Paul Lee Tan (Rockville, MD: Assurance Publishers, 1979), p. 1257.

[31]*Norman Vincent Peale's Treasury of Courage and Confidence*, Norman Vincent Peale (ed.) (NY: Doubleday and Co., 1970), pp. 289-290.

[32]*Reader's Digest*, April 1996, p. 185.

[33]*Encyclopedia of 7700 Illustrations*, Paul Lee Tan (Rockville, MD: Assurance Publishers, 1979), p. 131.

[34]*Guideposts*, July 1995, pp. 20-23.

[35]*Lessons from Mom*, Joan Aho Ryan (Deerfield Beach, FL: Health Communications, 1996), pp. 19-21.

[36]*Encyclopedia of 7700 Illustrations*, Paul Lee Tan (Rockville, MD: Assurance Publishers, 1979), p. 2068.

[37]*Norman Vincent Peak's Treasury of Courage and Confidence*, Norman Vincent Peale (ed.) (Garden City, NY: Doubleday and Co., 1970), pp. 269-271.

[38]*Reader's Digest*, July 1996, p. 48.

[39]*Knight's Treasury of 4,000 Illustrations*, Walter B. Knight (Grand Rapids, MI: Wm. B. Eerdmans Publishing Co., 1956. 1994), p. 167.

[40]*San Luis Obispo Telegram-Tribune*, September 16, 1996, B3.

[41]*Illustrations Unlimited*, James S. Hewett (Wheaton, IL: Tyndale, 1988), p. 226.

[42]*Encyclopedia of 7700 Illustrations*, Paul Lee Tan (Rockville, MD: Assurance Publishers, 1979), p. 759.

[43]*The Phoenix Factor*, Dr. Karl Slaikeu and Steve Lawhead (Boston, MA: Houghton Mifflin Co., 1985), p. 106-107.

[44]*Reader's Digest*, August 1995, p. 109-110.

[45]*Encyclopedia of 7700 Illustrations*, Paul Lee Tan (Rockville, MD: Assurance Publishers, 1979), p. 2077.

[46]*Sin, Sex, and Self-Control*, Norman Vincent Peale (NY: Doubleday and Co., 1965), p. 160-161.

[47]*Reader's Digest*, December 1992, pp. 9-12.

[48]*Encyclopedia of 7700 Illustrations*, Paul Lee Tan (Rockville, MD: Assurance Publishers, 1979), pp. 2041-2042.

[49]*Fruits of the Spirit*, Ron Hembree (Grand Rapids, MI: Baker Book House, 1969), pp. 72-73.

[50]*A 3rd Serving of Chicken Soup for the Soul*, Jack Canfield and Mark Victor Hansen (Deerfield Beach, FL: Health Communications, 1996), pp. 220-222.

[51]*Encyclopedia of 7700 Illustrations*, Paul Lee Tan (Rockville, MD: Assurance Publishers, 1979), pp. 2048.

[52]*You Can Make a Difference*, Earl Babbie (NY: St. Martin's Press, 1985), pp. 146-147.

[53]*Illustrations Unlimited*, James S. Hewett (Wheaton, IL: Tyndale, 1988), p. 206.

[54]*Encyclopedia of 7700 Illustrations*, Paul Lee Tan (Rockville, MD: Assurance Publishers, 1979), p. 1230.

[55]*A Man Called Peter*, Catherine Marshall (NY: Avon, 1971), pp. 168-169.

[56] *A 3rd Serving of Chicken Soup for the Soul*, Jack Canfield and Mark Victor Hansen (Deerfield Beach, FL: Health Communications, 1996), pp. 211-214.

[57] *Encyclopedia of 7700 Illustrations*, Paul Lee Tan (Rockville, MD: Assurance Publishers, 1979), pp. 361, 421-422.

[58] *The Best Loved Poems of the American People*, Hazel Felleman (NY: Doubleday. 1936), pp. 124-125. Stanzas 1, 3, and 6.

[59] *Life's Bottom Line*, Richard Exley (Tulsa, OK: Honor Books, 1990), p. 28.

[60] *Encyclopedia of 7700 Illustrations*, Paul Lee Tan (Rockville, MD: Assurance Publishers, 1979), p. 2066.

[61] *Discoveries*, Eugenia Price (Grand Rapids, MI: Zondervan Publishing House, 1953, 1970), pp. 32-33.

[62] *Illustrations Unlimited*, James S. Hewett (Wheaton, IL: Tyndale, 1988), pp. 348, 352.

[63] *Illustrations for Preaching and Teaching*, Craig Brian Larson (ed.), (Grand Rapids, MI: Baker Books, 1993), p. 156.

[64] *Growing Strong in the Seasons of Life*, Charles R. Swindoll (Portland, OR: Multnomah Press, 1983), p. 133.

[65] *A 2nd Helping of Chicken Soup for the Soul,* Jack Canfield and Mark Victor Hansen (Deerfield Beach, FL: Health Communications, 1995), pp. 46-48.

[66] *Illustrations for Preaching and Teaching*, Craig Brian Larson (ed.), (Grand Rapids, MI: Baker Books, 1993), p. 127.

[67] *The New Dynamics of Winning*, Denis Waitley, (NY: William Morrow & Co., 1993), pp. 171-172.

[68] *Illustrations Unlimited*, James S. Hewett (Wheaton, IL: Tyndale, 1988), p. 361-362.

[69] *Encyclopedia of 7700 Illustrations*, Paul Lee Tan (Rockville, MD: Assurance Publishers, 1979), p. 1506.

[70]*Against the Night*, Charles Colson with Ellen Santilli Vaughn (Ann Arbor. MI: Servant Publications, 1989), pp. 176-177.

[71]*Reader's Digest*, May 1995, p. 46.

[72]*Knights Treasury of 4,000 Illustrations*, Walter B. Knight (Grand Rapids, MI: W. B. Eerdmans Publishing Co., 1956, 1994), p. 520.

[73]*You Learn by Living*, Eleanor Roosevelt (NY: Harper & Brothers, 1960), pp. 26-27.

[74]*Illustrations Unlimited*, James S. Hewett (Wheaton, IL: Tyndale. 1988), pp. 55-56.

[75]*Encyclopedia of 7700 Illustrations*, Paul Lee Tan (Rockville, MD: Assurance Publishers, 1979), p. 2066.

[76]*Rock-Solid Marriage*, Robert and Rosemary Barnes (Dallas, TX: Word Publishing, 1993), p. 53.

[77]*Reader's Digest*, April 1996, pp. 71-76.

[78]*Encyclopedia of 7700 Illustrations*, Paul Lee Tan (Rockville, MD: Assurance Publishers, 1979), pp. 458-459.

[79]*Deep Down*, Tom Riter (Wheaton, IL: Tyndale House, 1995), p. 85.

[80]*Readers Digest*, November 1996, pp. 19-24.

[81]*Encyclopedia of 7700 Illustrations*. Paul Lee Tan (Rockville, MD: Assurance Publishers, 1979), pp. 737-738.

[82]*The Body*, Charles Colson with Ellen Santilli Vaughn (Dallas, TX: Word Publishing, 1992), pp. 325-326.

[83]*Illustrations Unlimited*, James S. Hewett (Wheaton, IL: Tyndale, 1988), pp. 24-25.

[84]*Encyclopedia of 7700 Illustrations*. Paul Lee Tan (Rockville, MD: Assurance Publishers, 1979), p. 294.

[85]*Sin, Sex, and Self-Control*, Norman Vincent Peale (NY: Doubleday & Co., 1965), pp. 195-197.

[86]*Mentors, Masters, and Mrs. MacGregor,* Jane Bluestlein (ed.) (Deerfield Beach, FL: Health Communications, 1995), pp. 12-13.

[87]*Encyclopedia of 7700 Illustrations.* Paul Lee Tan (Rockville, MD: Assurance Publishers, 1979), p. 2056.

[88]*The Body,* Charles Colson with Ellen Santilli Vaughn (Dallas, TX: Word Publishing, 1992), pp. 364-365.

[89]*Illustrations Unlimited,* James S. Hewett, (Wheaton, IL: Tyndale, 1988), p. 220.

[90]*Encyclopedia of Sermon Illustrations,* David F Burgess (St. Louis, MO: Concordia Publishing House, 1984), pp. 143-144.

[91]*You Can Make a Difference,* Earl Babbie (NY: St. Martins Press, 1985), pp. 5-6.

[92]*Illustrations Unlimited,* James S. Hewett (Wheaton, IL: Tyndale, 1988), pp. 413-414.

[93]*Encyclopedia of 7700 Illustrations,* Paul Lee Tan (Rockville, MD: Assurance Publishers, 1979), p. 2038.

[94]*Little House in the Ozarks* by Laura Ingalls Wilder, Stephen W. Hines (ed.) (Nashville, TN: Thomas Nelson Publishers, 1991). p. 296.

[95]*Readers Digest.* May 1996, pp. 169-172.

[96]*Encyclopedia of 7700 Illustrations,* Paul Lee Tan (Rockville, MD: Assurance Publishers, 1979), pp. 1499-1500.

[97]*First Things First,* Stephen R. Covey. A. Roger Merrill, Rebecca R. Merrill (NY: Simon & Schuster, 1994), pp. 65-67.

[98]*Readers Digest,* March 1995, p. 38.

[99]*Encyclopedia of Sermon Illustrations,* David E Burgess (St. Louis, MO: Concordia Publishing House, 1984), p. 78.

[100]*The Secret Garden,* Frances Hodgson Burnett (NY: Dell Publishing, 1911).

[101]*From Bad Beginnings to Happy Endings.* Ed Young (Nashville, TN: Thomas Nelson, 1994), p. 107.

[102]*Encyclopedia of 7700 Illustrations,* Paul Lee Tan (Rockville, MD: Assurance Publishers, 1979), pp. 2047-2048.

[103]*The Road to Faith,* Will Oursler (NY: Rinehart & Co., 1960). pp. 98-99.

[104]*From Bad Beginnings to Happy Endings.* Ed Young (Nashville, TN: Thomas Nelson, 1994), pp. 168-169.

[105]*Encyclopedia of 7700 Illustrations,* Paul Lee Tan (Rockville, MD: Assurance Publishers, 1979), pp. 2051-2052.

[106]*Deep Down,* Tom Riter (Wheaton, IL: Tyndale House, 1995), pp. 125, 130.

[107]*Mentors, Masters, and Mrs. MacGregor,* Jane Bluestein (ed.) (Deerfield Beach, FL: Health Communications, 1995), p. 59.

[108]*Encyclopedia of 7700 Illustrations,* Paul Lee Tan (Rockville, MD: Assurance Publishers, 1979), p. 2044.

[109]*Norman Vincent Peak's Treasury of Courage and Confidence,* Norman Vincent Peale (Garden City, NY: Doubleday & Co., 1970), pp. 6-7.

[110]*Illustrations Unlimited,* James S. Hewett (Wheaton, IL: Tyndale, 1988), pp. 446-447.

[111]*Encyclopedia of 7700 Illustrations,* Paul Lee Tan (Rockville, MD: Assurance Publishers, 1979), p. 2044.

[112]*San Luis Obispo Telegram-Tribune*, October 14, 1996, p. A7.

[113]*Reader's Digest*, April 1996, p. 42.

[114]*Illustrations Unlimited,* James S. Hewett (Wheaton, IL: Tyndale, 1988), p. 288.

[115]*Encyclopedia of 7700 Illustrations,* Paul Lee Tan (Rockville, MD: Assurance Publishers, 1979), p 1360.

[116]*Guideposts*, October 1996, pp. 18-20.

[117]*Illustrations Unlimited, James S. Hewett* (Wheaton, IL: Tyndale, 1988), p. 189.

[118]*Encyclopedia of 7700 Illustrations*, Paul Lee Tan (Rockville, MD: Assurance Publishers, 1979), p. 2067.

[119]*A Shepherd's Look at Psalm 23*, Phillip Keller (Irving, TX: Word, Inc., 1970), p. 24-26.

[120]*Illustrations Unlimited*, James S. Hewett (Wheaton, IL: Tyndale, 1988), p. 178.

[121]*Knight's Treasury of 2,000 Illustrations*, Walter B. Knight (Grand Rapids, MI: Wm. B. Eerdmans Publishing Co., 1963), pp. 70-71.

[122]*From Bad Beginnings to Happy Endings*, Ed Young (Nashville, TN: Thomas Nelson Publishers, 1994, p. 83.

[123]*Values From the Heartland*, Bettie B. Youngs (Deerfield Beach, FL: Health Communications, 1994, pp. 141-142.

[124]*Encyclopedia of 7700 Illustrations*, Paul Lee Tan (Rockville, MD: Assurance Publishers, 1979) p. 2072.

[125]*How to Change Your Spouse*, H. Norman Wright and Gary J. Oliver (Ann Arbor, MI: Servant Publications, 1994), p. 224.

[126]*Reader's Digest*, November 1996, pp. 133-134.

[127]*Encyclopedia of 7700 Illustrations*, Paul Lee Tan (Rockville, Md., Assurance Publishers, 1979), p. 399.

[128]*Getting Back on Track*, Dr. Bob Moorehead (Gresham, OR: Vision House Publishing, 1996), pp. 85-86.

[129]*Illustrations Unlimited*, James S. Hewett (Wheaton, IL: Tyndale, 1988), p. 128.

[130]*Encyclopedia of 7700 Illustrations*, Paul Lee Tan (Rockville, MD: Assurance Publishers, 1979), p. 2082.

[131]*Earl Nightingale's Greatest Discovery*, Earl C. Nightin-

gale (NY: Dodd, Mead &r Co., 1987), pp. 98-99.

[132]*Illustrations Unlimited,* James S. Hewett (Wheaton, IL: Tyndale, 1988), pp. 461-462.

[133]*Encyclopedia of 7700 Illustrations,* Paul Lee Tan (Rockville, MD: Assurance Publishers), pp. 2067, 2043.

[134]*From Bad Beginnings to Happy Endings,* Ed Young (Nashville, TN: Thomas Nelson Publishers, 1994), pp. 79-80.

[135]*Illustrations Unlimited,* James S. Hewett (Wheaton, IL: Tyndale, 1988), p. 347.

[136]*Encyclopedia of 7700 Illustrations,* Paul Lee Tan (Rockville, MD: Assurance Publishers, 1979), pp. 2054-2055.

[137]*San Luis Obispo Telegram-Tribune,* September 14, 1996, p. A4.

[138]*Illustrations Unlimited,* James S. Hewett (Wheaton, IL: Tyndale, 1988), p. 192.

[139]*Encyclopedia of 7700 Illustrations,* Paul Lee Tan (Rockville, MD: Assurance Publishers, 1979), p. 2037.

[140]*The 10 Natural Laws of Successful Time and Life Management,* Hyrum W. Smith (NY: Warner Books, 1994), pp. 23-24.

[141]*Illustrations Unlimited,* James S. Hewett (Wheaton, IL: Tyndale, 1988), pp. 366-367.

[142]*Encyclopedia of 7700 Illustrations,* Paul Lee Tan (Rockville, MD: Assurance Publishers, 1979), pp. 2052-2053.

[143]*The Seven Habits of Highly Effective People,* Stephen R. Covey (NY: Simon & Schuster, 1989), p. 142

[144]*A 3rd Serving of Chicken Soup for the Soul,* Jack Canfield and Mark Victor Hansen (Deerfield Beach, FL: Health Communications, 1996), pp. 278-282.

[145]*Illustrations for Preaching and Teaching,* Craig Brian

Larson (ed.) (Grand Rapids, MI: Baker Books, 1993), p. 248.

[146]*Uncommon Adventures,* Mark A. Tabb (Chicago, IL: Moody Press, 1995), p. 82.

[147]*A 3rd Serving of Chicken Soup for the Soul,* Jack Canfield and Mark Victor Hansen (Deerfield Beach, FL: Health Communications, 1996), pp. 245-246.

[148]*Encyclopedia of 7700 Illustrations,* Paul Lee Tan (Rockville, MD: Assurance Publishers, 1979), p. 335.

[149]*Uncommon Adventures,* Mark A. Tabb (Chicago, IL: Moody Press, 1995), p. 167.

[150]*A 3rd Serving of Chicken Soup for the Soul.* Jack Canfield and Mark Victor Hansen (Deerfield Beach, FL: Health Communications, 1996). pp. 307-312.

[151]*Encyclopedia of 7700 Illustrations,* Paul Lee Tan (Rockville, MD: Assurance Publishers, 1979), p. 2034.

[152]*Deep Down,* Tom Riter (Wheaton, IL: Tyndale House, 1995), p. 51.

[153]*Reader's Digest,* November 1996, p. 113.

[154]*Encyclopedia of 7700 Illustrations,* Paul Lee Tan (Rockville, MD: Assurance Publishers, 1979), p. 1232.

Additional copies of this book and other titles in the *God's Little Devotional Book* series are available at your local bookstore.

God's Little Devotional Book
God's Little Devotional Book for the Workplace
God's Little Devotional Book for Moms
God's Little Devotional Book for Dads
God's Little Devotional Book for Couples
God's Little Devotional Book for Men
God's Little Devotional Book for Women
God's Little Devotional Book for Parents
God's Little Devotional Book for Leaders
God's Little Devotional Book for Students
God's Little Devotional Book on Success
God's Little Devotional Book on Prayer
God's Little Devotional Book for Graduates